Under His Wings

and other places of refuge

Under His Wings

and other places of refuge

PATSY CLAIRMONT

PUBLISHING

Colorado Springs, Colorado

ISBN 1-56179-351-5

Published by Focus on the Family Publishing,
Colorado Springs, CO 80995.

Distributed in the U.S.A. and Canada by Word Books, Dallas, Texas.

Unless otherwise noted, Scripture quotations are from the *New
American Standard Bible*, copyright © 1960, 1963, 1968, 1971, 1973,
1975, and 1977 by The Lockman Foundation. Used by permission.
Those identified as NIV are from the HOLY BIBLE, NEW INTERNA-
TIONAL VERSION ®. Copyright © 1973, 1978, and 1984 by the
International Bible Society.
Used by permission of Zondervan Publishing House.
All rights reserved.

Editors: Janet Kobobel
        Larry K. Weeden
Cover design: Jeff Stoddard

Printed in the United States of America
94 95 96 97 98/10 9 8 7 6 5 4 3 2 1

Thank You, Lord, for making room for those who scamper under Your wings . . . just in time.

In memory of:

My dad,
Smith W. McEuen
1912-1979

My brother,
Donald C. McEuen
1936-1975

My godson,
Jeffrey D. Porter
1967-1994

Contents

Acknowledgments

Picture an unmade bed. That's what my manuscript looked like when I was working on it. All the components were there, but it wasn't very inviting. Janet Kobobel shook the sheets, fluffed the pillows, and smoothed out the spread, helping to transform this book into a more hospitable and comforting environment. Janet, you are a joy as a co-worker and have made the position of editor a term of endearment.

Mary Lou Schneemann, how grateful I am that you continue to offer your trained computer brain! Thanks for giving your expertise with patience and grace.

Sandra Fraley, what a gift you have been! I appreciate your hours of searching out permissions in the midst of your own challenging schedule.

I have surely been blessed with a plethora of friends. Eleanor Barzler, your sagacity and friendship are inspiring. Thanks also to Carol Porter, Ginny Lukei, Jan Frank, Lauren Heff, Lana Bateman, Debbie Wirwille, Danya Voigt, Lisa Harper, and Nancy and David Berrens. You all, in your own creative ways, cheer me on.

Mickey Mangun, Mary Hermes, and Jessica Shaver, thank you for sharing your tender and telling song and poems. Don Frank, I admire your gentle heart. Thank you for revealing it to us from your journal.

Thanks to my Focus family for believing in me.

Special thanks to Al Janssen, who listens to me with interest and responds with sensitivity and good humor. Larry Weeden, thank you for your tender touch-ups. Nancy Wallace, I appreciate your enthusiastic response to my efforts. Thanks also to Bev Rykerd, who is such fun to work with even when I'm not.

Mom, I continue to be indebted to you for your prayer coverage on my behalf.

Marty and Jason, I know I can no longer tuck you under my wings, but I pray you will both always take refuge under His wings.

Les, for the 32 years we've been married, you have, more times than I can count, extended to me your protection, comfort, and love. Your confidence in me has often been the impetus the Lord has used to keep me going. I am deeply moved by your servant's heart toward Him and me. I love you.

Chapter 1

Seeking Sanctuary

My friend Ann Downing has a singing style that causes my toes to tap and my heart to dance. Her voice is full of celebration. Included in Ann's repertoire are knee-slappin' songs as well as tear-dabbin' ones. One selection she often includes in her country performances (my tear-dabbin' favorite) is "The Long and Winding Road," by Mickey Mangun. My favorite line in that song is,

> *"I know I must be traveling right*
> *because I remember*
> *passing Calvary."*

For years I stumbled around emotionally, hiding in different places. Feeling overwhelmed by even the dailiness of life, I tried to find comfort and safety in the shelter of family members, friends, and activities. I drifted in a world full of panic—serious, unrelenting panic that held me hostage in my home for several years.

> *". . . my strength completely drained,*
> *I guess my face marks the pain,*
> *my back is bent from the strain."*

I retreated into my house to evade people and pressures; I longed for a safe place. Yet I couldn't escape my inner anxiety. I would wake up tense. Days felt more like weeks, and nights were full of fear. I slept too much. I ate too much. I talked too much. I was into unhealthy swings of muchness.

Then I remembered passing Calvary. That reminder helped me eventually to give up my shaky shelters that I might seek refuge in a much more secure place—under God's wings. Since then I have learned that we hide because we hurt, and we hurt because we don't understand how to heal. That's part of what this book is about, uncovering the places we hide and discovering how we can be healed. Healed from what? Healed from the wounds caused by anger, neglect, lies, and other forms of personal injury that we all struggle with to some degree.

> *"I covered many miles behind me,*
> *miles of sun and rain,*
> *and miles of smiles and pain."*

Today I am no longer housebound, I'm airborne. I travel throughout the country offering encouragement to others who are struggling emotionally. I meet folks who just need someone to validate what they're feeling. Some are stuck in unforgiveness and need help to pull free. Most are not as severely damaged as I was, but others are in even greater emotional dilemmas. I am not a professional (except in being a cracked pot), but I have learned and am learning insights regarding emotional unsteadiness, how we become frail, and how we can become stronger and more balanced.

> *"Up ahead I see a sign*
> *that points me*
> *straight ahead*
> *to victory."*

Travel with me down the winding road to emotional well-being. It's a road similar to the one the Israelites walked on their way to the promised land, which means we may uncover some giants, a plague or two, and a few pits. But we will also climb mountains, munch manna, and, with His help, gain some life-changing views.

> *"I really can't turn back,*
> *some may be using my tracks."*

This won't be a quick trip, so you may want to bring your luggage. Fill the suitcase with your honesty, some vulnerability, and a lot of tenacity.

> *"There are some times when*

the rocks hurt my feet
my body burns from the sweat
and the heat."

We will have the opportunity along the way to laugh, cry, grieve, and celebrate as we examine and adjust our reactions to life and people.

"Although it's dusty and old
for years it's borne
the traveler's load
and one day this road
will turn to gold."

Most importantly, we will respond to truth by putting one foot in front of the other as we move closer to the Savior and experience what it means to take sanctuary under His wings.

PART 1

HIDING

- *Hiders*
- *Hideouts*
- *Hidden Agendas*

Chapter 2

Hiders

Adam and Eve ducked behind the tattletale tree when they sinned, and we've been playing hide-and-seek ever since.

The tattletale couple later gave birth to a temper-tantrum son. Cain, however, unlike his parents, didn't blame. No, his was a more deadly game—killing his brother. Cain hid his murderous deed behind a lie and lost everything he loved most. Then, like his parents, he received an eviction notice. He was sent away from the harvest of the land and the fullness of God's presence.

Cain knew what was expected of him, but . . . Cain

wasn't able. He wasn't willing to relinquish his rights and submit to the ways of God, so he hid.

Truth be known, any one of our names could appear as a Peekaboo Profile, for we all have tried to cover up, cloud over, or camouflage our footprints at one time or another.

The fall of man brought with it shame, which has made hiding in the shadows easier than walking in the light. Ask Cain. Or David. Or Jonah or Elijah . . . or Judas!

Check out Jonah, the Joppa Jogger. Jonah chose napping in the basement of a boat over trumpeting truth to Nineveh and ended up bait on his own hook.

And look at Elijah, who hid out in a stone fortress. He didn't stand fast; he *ran* fast and ended up caving in.

King David didn't cave in; he *craved* in. His desires for the bathing beauty next door infected his royal judgment, and instead of marching off to battle, he sashayed with his neighbor into his bedroom. And like Bathsheba's bubble soap, David ended up in hot water.

Sheltering in his lover's arms set up King David to become one of Cain's Commandos. To disguise his lack of integrity, David, too, bumped off his "brother."

Whether in a garden, a gangway, a grotto, or a game with a gal, from the beginning God's people have played the fugitive as they ran from one hiding place to another. And today, when we dart off in the wrong direction, we, too, feel the hot breath of the enemy on our collars. For it is in the dark crannies that Ol' Beelzebub carries out his revolt.

But there is One who sees our game-playing exhaustion and longs for us to know His rest. He understands our desire for a hiding place. He woos us to His soothing side—even when it's Him we've foolishly been hiding from—so that we might find the refuge we so desperately need.

The way to His holy habitat is a path of light. That can be a problem if our eyes have become acclimated to the shadows of game playing. We will tend to pull back from the first painful light of illumination. But just as we adjusted to the deception, so we can choose to adapt to the light and thereby move closer to the Truth.

Let's begin by looking at a few profiles from *Who's Who of Peekaboo* to gain some insights on hiding.

Moses was plunged into his first game of peekaboo with his sister, Miriam. To save his life, his mom tucked Moses into a basket and then slipped him into the Nile. Miriam peeked at Moses from her hiding place, as her little brother's bassinet bobbed between the bulrushes. Baby Moses didn't like this game of peekaboo and bellowed his protest.

At that moment, Pharaoh's daughter, who was doing her morning aerobics on the riverbank, spotted the covered container. Upon lifting the lid, the Egyptian princess found the little basket case and wanted him for her own. She decided to raise her newfound water baby in the palace as a prince.

Funny thing, Moses didn't prize princeship any better than he liked peekaboo. And in an adult moment of childish fury, he took up bushwhacking when he bumped off an Egyptian to protect his Hebrew brothers. Evidently Moses thought hiding had worked for him once, so he would try it again. He then stashed the Egyptian's body under the shifting sand.

Well, the sand didn't shift, but Moses' favor did. When Grandpappy Pharaoh found out about Moses' dastardly deed, he dropped Moses from his will and sent out a posse to finish him off.

Moses was too big to hide in the reeds, so he set off on his steed across the searing sands and eventually ended up at the burning bush.

Barefoot and now bashful, Moses had given up bush-whacking and taken up benchwarming. Instead of finding warmth in the fire of the Lord, Moses wrapped up in a blanket of cozy excuses. Seems the Lord had a plan for this ex-basket case/bushwhacker that didn't appeal to Moses. Talk about a job placement nightmare! Moses just couldn't find his niche. But he did think his brother, Aaron, could handle this Dale Carnegie opportunity to be God's spokesman to Pharaoh. And that's how Moses advised the Lord.

I guess Moses had become so used to tending sheep that he forgot he was one. Instead of listening to the Shepherd, Moses stood on his warm bench and covered himself with his protests.

Hmm, isn't that where Moses started off his life . . . protesting? What a whiner!

So then how did Moses end up such a winner? Certainly not by being a basket case, a bushwhacker, or a benchwarmer. Those were all temporary, ineffective human efforts to find shelter. No, Moses moved into the winner's circle when he became a bondsman. He offered himself as human collateral for God's people.

Somewhere on the path to the promised land, this prophet gave up his childish cover-ups and took up righteous refuging. Moses didn't run away and hide, but instead, when things got tough, he offered his life as a sacrifice (in place of the Hebrew hellions).

The Lord responded and placed Moses in the cleft of a rock and sheltered him under His hand. The Lord hid Moses from His glory (which would have killed him) and exposed him to His goodness (which instead filled him). The change in Moses was so startling that he became a literal beacon in his neighborhood. By popular demand, he had to veil his face as it continued to reflect his holy Hiding Place—which scared the daylights out of his shady followers.

Here was a job hopper who went from thinking he couldn't converse with men to talking "face to face" with God. Wow, that gives me hope!

Of course, it's not as though Moses walked from that time forward in all the light he had. (But then, who does?) At one point, he refuged in his rights instead of the Lord's might when he found himself between a rock (the Lord) and a hard place (the people). Instead of speaking up, he literally struck out by hitting the rock and then taking credit for the water that sprang from it.

Yet his life did end with a mountaintop experience. Concealed from the view of the people, God showed

Moses, atop Mount Nebo, what none of them had seen—
the promised land. After 120 years of hiding in one way or
another, Moses died . . . and God hid his body.

Moses went from being hidden at birth by his earthly
mother to being hidden at death by his heavenly Father.

"Since then, no prophet has risen in Israel like Moses,
whom the LORD knew face to face" (Deut. 34:10, NIV).

Moses' theme song could have been "Na, na, na, can't
find me!" But then I, too, could have sung it without missing a beat. I can't begin to tell you how many times I've felt
like a basket case and wanted to hide. Often I behaved out
of the emotions of an abandoned child. I referred to myself
as "deeply sensitive." The truth is I wore my feelings on my
fingertips and then cried like a baby if you touched them.
Talk about a whiner! Not only did I whine well (Mom
always said that if you're going to do something, do it
well), but I also could have given Moses some pointers on
pouting—that is, if I wasn't too busy shouting.

Now, I have never bumped off anyone like our bush-
whacking friend, but if words were bullets, I'd hate to
count the bodies I'd have left strewn in the path of my life.
You see, shooting off one's mouth wounds those around
us. Misdirected anger always leaves victims. When I finally
learned to shut up and sit down, I got so comfortable I
didn't want to get up again. As a benchwarmer, I sat down
so hard and for so long that I became a trenchwarmer. It
was difficult for me to change after I became entrenched in
my misery. Not that I liked my pain, but the price of
change was great, and I wasn't sure I could pay it. Besides,
my instability had already cost me so much that I felt too

low on funds to afford a new lease on life.

So you see, Moses' responses are not antiquated but are applicable to any of us who have ever felt deserted, misunderstood, or too inadequate to be used by God. His story gives me hope, because Moses wasn't an overnight wonder. He stumbled and grumbled just as I did—and still do at times. Yet eventually he found his way to the mountaintop and, more importantly, into the sheltering presence of the Lord.

In time, Moses gave up "Na, na, na," and I believe he learned to sing a new song:

"Rock of Ages cleft for me,
let me hide myself in Thee."

Thanks, Moses, for helping us to see that we have a choice about where we hide and that our hiding place will determine the quality and dignity of our life's song.

It's hard to sing, even the blues, when your future looks black. Color Hagar's emotions black and blue from the hard knocks life dealt her. How did this bruised young woman finally find refuge for her son and herself that ended the abuse and gave them a promising future?

I wonder if the name *Hagar* means "wrung out and hung up to dry"? Sarai must have thought so, for she not only twisted Hagar's emotions into knots with her tyranny, but she also sent Hagar scurrying into the desert to dry out . . . or up. This gal Hagar knew what it was like to be abused, intimidated, rejected, and deserted. No wonder she took up hiding.

Hagar was an Egyptian girl selected to be Sarai's hand-maiden. Now, she didn't volunteer for the job or answer a want ad. Nor was she directed to it by a career counselor. No, we are talking about a decree. But for Hagar, it felt more like "degree" when Sarai turned up the heat of her anger and tried to turn Hagar's future into desert dust.

Not once but twice, Sarai sent Hagar hot-footing it across the sands looking for an oasis. The first time, Hagar wanted a place to hide where her hormonal boss wouldn't find her and erupt again. And who could blame her?

Of course, the handmaiden hadn't helped things when she had snubbed her boss because she was preg-nant and Sarai wasn't. Sarai's response reminds me of the old margarine commercials in which Mother Nature proclaims, "It's not nice to fool Mother Nature!" And in one whisk of her wand, she wipes out half the forest. Hagar wished she had sought refuge in a forest—at least there she could have taken shelter under a shady tree.

Instead, she found herself weeping at a desert spring. Her tears, I'm sure, were intermingled with anguish at the rage of Sarai, as well as with personal regret for being spite-ful. In that lonely moment, an angel appeared and instructed Hagar to swallow her pride (talk about indiges-tion), give up her hiding place (talk about vulnerability), and return to her old job (talk about boring).

No doubt motivated by the angel's prediction of a

promising future for her coming child, Hagar returned to Sarai's encampment. After the birth of her son, she must have maintained a low profile, because we don't hear about her again for some time. Perhaps she sheltered in the angel's promise.

Years passed, and Sarai's life changed. She received a new name, Sarah, and she gave birth to a son at the age of 90. (Talk about a change-of-life baby!) The child certainly did change Sarah's life, but not her disposition. For when Hagar's son, Ishmael, was caught teasing Sarah's son, Isaac, she had Hagar and Ishmael both booted out of the camp—forever.

I wonder if, when Hagar gave birth to Abraham's first child, she believed that she and her son would be physically and financially set for life, that they had found the perfect refuge. What a jolt, then, to have her child's father hand her some bread, a skin of water, and full responsibility for the rearing of their son. Abraham placed the provisions on her shoulders and evicted her. I'll bet the bread felt like lead as Hagar realized she was carrying her son's full inheritance—with no hope of child support.

Again Hagar ended up in the desert. Was she looking for the angel? Maybe not; after all, she had to doubt his prophetic credentials at that point. Yet a part of her wanted to believe that since God had met her in the desert once, perhaps He would again. When their prisoner's portion of bread and water was used up, this single mom and her child began to give up. The blistering sun had left them parched and pleading. Hagar hid her face from her dehydrated son. She could not bear to watch him die.

What happened next? Sure enough, the angel returned. (I wonder if angels always inhabit difficult terrain?) After a short exchange, God opened Hagar's eyes. The dust of disillusionment had blinded her, causing her to miss God's provision, which was in her midst all along . . . a desert well.

Well, well, well, what looked like the end was actually a new beginning for Hagar and Ishmael. Evidently Hagar found the wilderness an ideal place to seek refuge, because she and Ishmael set up housekeeping in Paran. His nomadic lifestyle as an archer suited his feisty character. And Mama Hagar fulfilled her dream when she returned home to Egypt and selected a wife for her son from her own people.

Who could have guessed that such hardship would become a highway in the wilderness? Never again would Hagar have to run away, hide away, or be thrown away at the whim of Sarah.

When Janice married Jim, she never suspected her lot in life would look a lot like Hagar's. Instead, Janice knew her marriage was forever. Both Jim's and Janice's parents had weathered matrimonial difficulties, and they strongly supported their children's marriage. Besides, the newly-weds were deeply in love.

Jim's parents, as a wedding gift, presented them with a key to a mortgage-free home. And Jim had landed a high position in a firm that put them in a financially secure place. So unlike most young couples, they didn't have to deal with a tight budget. They found their pressure-free relationship a safe place to refuge.

After the birth of their daughter, Tina, however, Janice noticed changes in Jim. At first he seemed preoccupied, then he distanced himself emotionally, and in time he became antagonistic.

Janice wondered if Jim was upset by the weight she'd kept on after Tina's birth. So she joined a morning aerobics class, hoping the toning of her body would improve the tone of her marriage. Then she thought maybe Jim wasn't ready to share her with the baby. So Janice's mom kept Tina overnight once a week to provide them with their own time.

But it seemed the more Janice tried, the more hateful Jim acted. Then one evening, he told her to get out of his house. Hurt and confused, she wrapped up the baby and drove around the block. After an hour of tears and feeling as though she had been sent out into the desert, she decided to go home and plead with Jim to tell her what she had done to make him so angry. But Jim refused to even let her in.

Not wanting anyone to know she had been thrown out of her home, Janice rented a motel room and waited for the lonely night to end. When she was sure Jim had left for work the next morning, she went home—only to find he had changed all the locks.

Janice returned to her parents' home. In the ensuing weeks, Jim gave the house back to his parents, quit his job, and left the country.

Grief-stricken and broke, Janice wandered in the

wilderness of despair. Feelings of failure and betrayal pushed her into hiding from others. Following in the sandalprints of Hagar, Janice fell under the weight of her own heart and wept. She cried for her fatherless child, she cried for her own humiliation, and she cried over the bleak future. Finally, at her parents' insistence, she agreed to talk with a counselor.

Janice still says that her counselor was an "angel" from the Lord. Unlike Hagar's angel, Janice's was human; but like Hagar's messenger, Janice's brought her comfort, hope, and light. She helped Janice to come out of unhealthy hiding and seek refuge in the Lord, and she opened Janice's eyes to see her circumstances more clearly. The counselor encouraged Janice to let go of what she couldn't change and to find, like Hagar, her own "well." Jim's choices didn't have to determine the quality and outcome of her future.

Janice didn't have a corner on hiding. For Jim not only fled the country to dodge his family responsibilities, but he also took along a secret handmaiden he had met at work.

Life often isn't fair. Ask the Hagars in this world who experience intimidation, rejection, abandonment, and the pangs of raising a child alone. I tried to look up *fair* in my concordance, and it just wasn't there.

Fair means "proper." It's a word that's mixed with human adjustments to try to satisfy all who are involved. When we try to serve equal portions of dessert at a birthday party or try to treat the Ishmaels and Isaacs in our lives equally, we want to be fair. But more often than not, we mismeasure.

Good news, however: God is just, which beats fair in the long run, hands up. *Just* means "righteous." It's a word that is pure and established on unchanging truth and ultimately serves our highest interest. *Ultimately* is a key word, because *just* is like a missing puzzle piece. We often search to fill the empty space, but when the hidden piece "ultimately" is found and set in place, the picture makes sense.

Ask Janice. Not that her way has always made sense to her, nor has it been easy, but her trust has been strengthened in the Just One who sees her even in the wilderness. And she knows that His justice frees her from hiding in the shadows of her losses so she can walk in the light—even when her throat is parched and her heart is broken.

Our next hider probably wouldn't have thought *broken* was a strong enough word to describe her condition. She might have suggested *shattered.* A woman left barren by loss, she eventually returned to the Harvester of hurting hearts.

Elimelech ("Elim") and Naomi had a decision to make. Times were tough, food was in short supply and diminishing rapidly, and the future in Bethlehem looked dismal. Elim and Naomi had two sons, Mahlon and Chilion, for whom they were concerned. After looking at the troubled economy and the community's limited provisions, Elim decided to shelter his family from the famine by moving to Moab.

I personally have never known hunger or been threatened by it, but my husband, Les, and I have known slim times. Our pantry has been full, but our pockets have been empty. We have suffered financial famine that left us searching for a way out. Les and I carefully evaluated our options so we could improve the quality of our lives as well as that of our sons.

I wonder if Elim and Naomi made a list of the positives and negatives for remaining in Bethlehem . . . or living in Moab. They may have created the first list, but I have my doubts about how well they thought through life with the Moabites. Of course, things like budgets, diets, and reasons to move always look more manageable on paper.

Les and I have moved 27 times in our 32 (and counting) years of marriage. Before each move, we weighed the impact on our children. I have no doubt that Elim and Naomi's desires for their family were as strong as ours, but, like us, they failed to see the full outcome of their decisions.

If you asked our firstborn what was the most difficult part of his growing-up years, Marty would tell you it was changing schools so often. Even though we stayed in the same community, he attended seven different schools, which he found not only difficult, but also painful.

If we could interview Mahlon or Chilion about their move, what do you think they might say was the hardest struggle for them? Perhaps that they were not only the new kids on the block, but that they also looked, talked, and behaved differently from the neighbors. Or that others were trying to convert them into followers of one of Moab's many gods. Then again, maybe Mahlon and Chilion thought their new surroundings were exciting and expanding—which, if true, actually presented a whole crop of other problems, ones that had the potential of breaking a mom and dad's heart.

Elimelech's name means "My God is king." If names are consistent with character, isn't it perplexing that Elim took refuge in the enemy's camp? The people of Moab came out of the incestuous relationship between drunken Lot and his scheming daughters. The Moabites had a history of idolatry and often warred against Israel. That seems to me like two strong reasons, especially when your name means "My God is king," to avoid Moab.

Following this line on names, how is it that "My God is king" and his wife, "pleasantness," raised two weak sons, Mahlon ("invalid") and Chilion ("pining")? Of course, who's to say? Those young men may have been physically handicapped, although it would seem their names referred to their personal character rather than their physical condition. Yet it's a medical fact that sustained emotional pain will cause physical disruptions.

It almost appears as though Elimelech and Naomi chose physical comforts over spiritual welfare for their sons. (Could that have been why they were weak?) Perhaps Elim thought his own strong faith would provide a fortress for his sons to hide in from the temptations that surrounded them. And maybe he *was* a protection for them. Of course, he probably had not planned on dying while in Moab, but he did. And that's one of the problems with having a human refuge: Sometimes that person leaves.

My husband's father was a powerful parental figure in mostly negative ways. In fact, he was Moab in britches. He was an abusive alcoholic who warred against everyone. He did provide definite boundaries for his six children, which in some ways protected them from young, foolish choices. But, like Elim, he had not counted on his own premature death. Les was left reeling emotionally. Viewing his dad's death as a license to live it up, Les let rowdy behavior cause him all kinds of problems.

Scripture records Elim's death in Ruth 1:3 and his sons' weddings to Moabite women in verse 4. Do you think Mahlon and Chilion's dad forbade them from making that choice while he was alive? And once he had died, Mrs. Pleasantness gave in to their desires? Just a thought.

As a mom of two sons, I confess I enjoy pleasing them and seeing them happy. And at times I, too, have been guilty of indulging some wishes that weren't in Marty and Jason's best interests—like loaning them money I knew I wouldn't get back, allowing them to stay up later than they should, or sheltering them from their father's displeasure when they needed to face his wrath. Yes, I guess I could understand if Naomi wavered when she should have stood fast . . . and I have learned, as Naomi may have, the error of indulgence.

Pining is defined as "to wither away from longing or grief." I wonder if Chilion's pining sprang up from the death of his dad. To lose a strong parental figure is not only jolting, but also emotionally disconcerting. Maybe the weighty loss of homeland and father was more than Chilion could bear. Perhaps he, like Les, was left reeling.

We don't know how much time elapsed between Elimelech's death and his sons' marriages, but within ten years after their dad died, so did Mahlon and Chilion.

Poor Naomi suffered tremendous loss in the land where they had sought safety. Elim and Naomi had intended to sojourn for a season and return to Bethlehem when the economy improved. But the seasons swirled by, and still they stayed.

Intentions. How many good ones I've had! "This will work," I surmise from my human calculations, only to learn later my prediction was myopic. I've always thought it would be great if we could Reebok down to the drug-store and purchase some spiritual Murine. A few drops in each eye and—presto!—20/20 insight and foresight.

The Scottish poet Robert Burns put it this way:

"The best laid schemes o' mice and men
Gang aft a-gley."

Bobby-boy reminds us that no matter how well we plan, life is brimming over with the "unexpecteds."

The unexpected battered Naomi's heart again and again. She was so bent over with grief that all her pleas-antness spilled out. And when she rose up from the third gravesite, having buried her husband and both sons, her bruised heart filled with bitterness.

Feet weighted with dread, Naomi trudged toward Moab's closest exit and beyond to Bethlehem. No star appeared over a stable to guide her home. Besides, her heart was too heavy to look up. She didn't even see the loving intentions of her daughters-in-law as they pursued her. Instead Naomi, wrapped tightly in her shroud of depression, tried to send them away.

Like Naomi, I sojourned in depression for many years. This nook of darkness gave me a place to hole up—which I desperately needed—but it also robbed me of what would enable me to clearly see myself and others . . . light. My brooding spirit alienated me from people. Likewise, Naomi, blinded by her pain, could see no future for herself or anyone associated with her.

When my 38-year-old brother died following a car accident, my pain came like great waves that threatened to drown me. At high tide, my friend Rose read me a psalm over the roar of my grief. The Spirit of God encircled me with one of the verses like a life preserver: "I would have despaired unless I had believed that I would see the goodness of the LORD in the land of the living" (Ps. 27:13).

Despairing Naomi, now accompanied by her daughter-in-law Ruth, made the journey home. Ruth tried to encircle Naomi with her promise of lifelong care, but this bereft mother and wife could hear only her own agonized heart. As Naomi embraced the unfairness of her losses, her pain turned to bitter blame.

Naomi's complaints about how the Almighty had afflicted her diminished as she experienced His benevolent care for her as a widow. Naomi had come home to the friendship of His people and home to the Redeemer of her heart. Even though she returned with resentment, He met her where she was, and then He helped her move to a better emotional place. As she pulled out of her pain and became part of the provision for Ruth, Naomi's bitterness seemed to fade gradually.

There's always a price to pay when we seek refuge in the camp of the enemy. The good news is that a Redeemer waits for us to return and take refuge in Him.

How tender of the Father to woo Naomi's barren life home at harvesttime. And what a harvest it was! Food for her table and fruit for her lap. For from the fruit of Ruth's womb came a grandchild to fill Naomi's aching arms and to mend her broken dreams. I believe adopted Grandma Naomi encircled this child in the shelter of her care and whispered to him of the Lord's goodness in the land of the living. And to think she cradled to her softened heart the grandfather of King David and an heir to the very throne of God!

You may not see these hide-and-seek stories exactly as I do, but I think you'll agree that Moses, Hagar, and Naomi show us what a human tendency it is to dash away from difficulties and dart behind less-than-honorable shelters.

I personally have always found it easier to peek at other peoples' lives and see what they did wrong than to check a mirror and capture my own inconsistent reflection. The fascinating thing about the Word of God is that we start off learning about Bible characters and end up with a view from His looking glass of *our* character . . . and some of us don't like what we see. We begin to realize that Moses, Hagar, and Naomi are not distant kin but actually our kissing cousins with hideout routines like ours. And I wonder if they're not part of the great cloud of witnesses who are cheering us on and longing for us to learn from their mistakes and triumphs. If we could hear them, what might they say?

I think Moses might call down to us to leave our man-made tents in the valley and come up higher so we, too, can gain a holier perspective and catch a glimpse of the promised land.

Hagar's encouragement, as she serves us a cool cup of refreshment from her well, would be that we don't have to hide from a wilderness experience. In fact, the driest, most deserted times of our lives can cause us to thirst for the Living Water and discover the well that never runs dry.

Naomi's compassionate hand might soothe our troubled brows as she helps us keep in mind the only One who can shelter the grief-stricken heart and fill our empty lives with meaning.

We are reminded by our three fellow journeyers that while it is not wrong to hide, *where* we hide can help us . . . or hurt us.

Many of my hiding places have been constructed of popular, readily available materials. They fit right into our materialistic, narcissistic, hedonistic society. That means I want too much too often, think of myself more frequently than I should, and often act as though I have the right to be constantly entertained by life. This approach leaves me self-seeking, self-centered, and self-absorbed.

Yuck! Like too much sugar, an overdose of self is sickening. Let's see if we can pinpoint a few self-indulgent havens you may be sharing with me.

Chapter 3

Hideouts

Correct me if I'm wrong, but are there not strip malls on every corner throughout the United States of America? Actually, I know there are, because I've been in them. At times, malls have been my hiding place. When I haven't wanted to deal with real life, I've gone off to pretend all is well and that a new bauble will fill the unconscious ache within.

Shopping is not wrong in and of itself. It's when I use it to try to escape painful emotions, difficult relationships, or personal responsibilities that I get in the most trouble. One thing about seeking sanctuary in a mall is I have lots of addictive company. Somehow, seeing others laden down with their own packages eases my guilt.

Once I stayed out of the malls for a whole month . . . and gained ten pounds. When I set aside my packages, I then made a beeline for the pantry. I guess my theory was that if I couldn't buy off my problems, I'd bury them under a barrage of groceries. Of course, then I had to go back to the mall to buy bigger clothes.

When I wasn't shopping or eating, I was sleeping. Like a lethargic ostrich with his head stuck in a hole in the ground, I jumped in bed and covered my head, trying to escape my cluttered emotions.

Some days I would head for the mall, have lunch with a friend, and then go home and take a nap. That's a hider's home run! But when you have to face real life, you discover you actually struck out.

All my hiding places are inadequate, but each offers a quick fix. For the moment it takes my mind off my pain, my relationships that need attention, or responsibilities that feel overwhelming. But long term, my hiding places complicate my issues.

Shopping, eating, and sleeping are obvious places one might go to hide. But let's look at some of the more covert crannies, the private patterns that even we don't always realize we are sheltering in.

In the 19 years I've been raising Jason, I have asked this question a bajillion times: "Jason, why didn't you clean up your room?"

The following are just a few of his bajillion responses:

"I got in too late."

"I lay down for a minute and fell asleep."

"It didn't look dirty to me."

"I like it this way."

"My friends were coming over, and we'd just mess it up again."

"I'm waiting for Jim to get here so he can help me."

"Oh, did you mean this week?"

Every mom has heard an avalanche of excuses rumble forth from the mouths of her offspring regarding why certain tasks remain undone. And as the kids try to do a snow job on us, we are busy shoveling through their reasons, looking for the truth.

Often we find at the bottom of the pile procrastination, laziness, rebellion, fear, a need for control, a misunderstanding of what's expected, or an unwillingness to pay the price. On careful examination, we realize their faulty excuses sound familiar. That's why you often hear a parent reply, "Nice try, kids, but it won't work. I tried that on my parents, too." In fact, some of us become so adept at using excuses that we carry this hiding place into our adult lives.

I met Jody at a retreat in New York. After I finished my opening message on attitudes, she pulled me aside to confess her struggle with her mother-in-law. I asked Jody what her mother-in-law did that upset her the most. Without hesitation, she rattled off a list of offenses worthy of life imprisonment without hope of parole. I asked why she didn't make some changes in their relationship so she wouldn't feel violated. From Jody's lips tumbled an avalanche of rehearsed excuses that kept her frozen out of more meaningful relating.

As inappropriate as her in-laws' behavior was, Jody's lack of initiative to do all she knew she could didn't help her or them. No matter what solutions I suggested, Jody had a reason they wouldn't work.

Her heart had frozen over toward her in-laws. That meant her husband often got the cold shoulder, and at times her children would suffer from cold snaps.

When she finally decided to leave her icy habitat of excuses, Jody had to shovel her way through forgiveness and dig new tunnels of communication. It was exhausting work, because offenses had piled up for many winters.

Jody realizes today that she waited so long to make changes in her family relationships that the way out seemed overwhelming, and she wasn't sure she wanted to work that hard. Besides, sheltering in excuses was easier and less intimidating than confronting and forgiving. But as she made an effort and saw progress, the remaining ice crystals on her heart melted.

This is not to suggest that her in-laws still don't try to hurl snowballs at Jody. (She changed; they didn't.) But now she knows how to duck and not participate in their cold war.

Jason and Jody's tendencies to hide behind excuses are as old as Eden and as current as Congress. Remember

Moses' job opportunity as the Lord's spokesperson? When Moses cleared his throat, it wasn't a speech that came out but a list of excuses.

Or ask Aaron. You know, Moses' brother. When he was confronted concerning the golden calf the Israelites were worshiping, Aaron said, "I threw it [gold] into the fire, and out came this calf" (Exod. 32:24). Oh, moo-ve over, Aaron; my kids could have been more creative than that.

Even courageous Queen Esther did a hesitation step behind a castle wall of excuses when Mordecai compelled her to plead for their people to the king. Seems the king wasn't too thrilled with uninvited guests and had a habit of bumping them off. (I've wanted to bump off a few myself, but it hasn't worked well for me. Instead I just cook for my guests, and funny thing . . . they leave.)

We may hide behind excuses, but ultimately, excuses eradicate personal growth.

Steven made people laugh even when they didn't want to. It wasn't that he always saw the best in a situation, but he did have a way of finding the humorous or the ridiculous. He was an outrageous sort of fellow. He wore comical hats, mismatched socks, and outlandish trousers. Steven was an unending vaudeville routine.

Real life banged hard on Steven's door when he lost his job, but he just laughed it off. A new position didn't come in time to save his home, but Steven proclaimed, "Easy come, easy go." Then a battering ram hit when his wife died, and it knocked the sense of humor right out of him.

It was a scary time for Steven. He had hid behind his humor to keep from feeling. Without that hiding place, he was exposed to a lifetime of emotions he had stuffed under his endless stream of jokes.

When Steven stopped laughing, his neglected emotions demanded attention. Anger, fear, jealousy, and other feelings crowded his awareness. This time, instead of denying their existence by laughing them away, he learned to identify his inner reactions.

Steven practiced saying how he felt in a support group and talked with others about how to handle his emotions. He embraced the importance of speaking the truth in love about how he felt.

As he gave himself permission to feel and learned how to express his feelings appropriately, Steven began to heal. Naming his feelings was the first step in getting a grip on reality. It started him on a healthy journey of self-discovery that eventually led to recovery. His emotional restoration didn't eliminate his sense of humor—it balanced it.

Most of us don't use hand buzzers or exploding cigars, but we have been guilty of laughing about something that not only wasn't funny, but also wounded us or someone else. We usually chuckle to cover our pain or embarrassment. Our face says "funny" while our heart says "ouch."

Humor acts like a gate—it makes us appear friendly while preventing accessibility, lest when others enter they see our deep sense of inadequacy. We have all heard rotund people make fun of their size when the truth is they'd give anything to lose weight. Or petite people who tell short jokes while the lifts on their shoes make a grandiose statement of their own. Self-debasing humor is often an attempt to beat others to the punch, giving us a sense of control over our own shortcomings.

I have always looked older than my age. When I was young, it was great. But guess what? I'm not that young anymore, and it's not great to hear others guess that I'm ten to 15 years older than I am. I found myself doing elderly jokes about my ancient appearance before people could hurt my feelings.

"I spent five hours at the beauty parlor today . . . and that was just for an estimate," I'd quip à la Phyllis Diller.

Then I realized how dishonest that was. I was pretending it didn't bother me when it did. To lie about my feelings was to lock myself in a closet of taunting mirrors. So I started to tell my audiences what a sensitive issue my older appearance was for me. My confession didn't stop all the insensitive comments, but it helped me to become more honest. As I stepped from behind the gate of my unhealthy humor, I began to heal. That left me less likely to be devastated the next time someone wondered if I was Methuselah's mother. I learned that when our humor is forced, it's not healthy.

Hurling humor like hand grenades is a popular sport today. We think it's acceptable to pull the pin on our anger as long as we toss it in a casing of humor. The problem is it's still explosive, and someone ends up hurt. And as the victims of our gibing pick shrapnel out of their self-esteem, we accuse them of not having a sense of humor. The truth is, we haven't been willing to face our TNT personality, which has left us combustible comedians with machine-gun mouths.

How many times have you heard or said, "I was only kidding"? If we have to defend our humor regularly, chances are we're not as funny as we may think. When our defense mechanisms go up, our hearing ability goes down. We become so busy building a wall to hide behind that we block out the legitimate protests of others.

Next time you think you've told a "funny," look around to see if anyone else is laughing. Grimaces don't count. If our humor turns out to be a solo act, we need to give it up before our comedy turns into a tragedy. For when we lose the respect of someone we care about, it is a tragedy.

A good humor rule is, if it hurts someone, it isn't funny. Again, if it hurts someone—anyone—it isn't funny. I have had to apologize more than once to individuals for using convenient humor, at their expense, to win the favor of others. Just because people are laughing doesn't mean what we said or did was appropriate or loving.

The enemy didn't give us our sense of humor, but he does work at perverting it. And we assist in the distortion when we use humor as a hideout from tender, honest relationships.

A healthy sense of humor is a precious gift given to promote good news, good health, and goodwill.

Maybe shopping, eating, sleeping, procrastinating, or

guffawing aren't the places you hide in. We are a creative group, and therefore lots of other options are out there. Your hiding place is wherever you run when the first inkling of feeling hurt crops up. And chances are it's a self-indulgent spot rather than a self-revealing one, which is why God is beckoning you to come out of hiding, into the light, and to slip under His comforting wings.

Chapter 4

Hidden Agendas

When Julie received the call from Andrea, she was delighted. They hadn't spoken for many months because of a misunderstanding. Julie was heartbroken over the rift, because she and Andrea had been close friends, or so she had thought. But when weeks turned into months and still Andrea hadn't talked to Julie, she began to give up on their reconciliation.

When Andrea did call, she sounded a little distant, but Julie didn't mind; she was just pleased to hear Andrea's voice. Andrea asked Julie to meet her for lunch, suggesting a restaurant on the other side of town. That surprised Julie a little, but she quickly put that thought aside and hurried to get ready.

During the drive, Julie began to reminisce. She laughed aloud several times as she thought of fun memories she and Andrea had shared. By the time she pulled into the restaurant parking area, she was singing.

She almost skipped into the lobby and quickly scanned the booths looking for her friend. Andrea leaned from her booth and waved to her. When Julie reached the table, she was startled to find a third party present. She tried not to look disappointed, but Julie wasn't prepared to share this time, especially with Lyndie.

Lyndie was a newcomer in their community and at their church. She seemed outgoing enough, but she had a haughty air that troubled Julie. Andrea and Lyndie, though, had hit it off. Julie was surprised since Andrea had never cared for uppity people before.

Feeling awkward, Julie forced a smile and slid into the booth. They exchanged a short round of pleasantries, placed their orders, and then sat in silence. Andrea's voice broke through the strained air. "You're probably wondering why I asked you to lunch," she said.

Julie looked at the two gals and realized this was a setup. These women knew exactly why they were there; it was Julie who was in the dark. She had fallen victim to their hidden agenda.

Andrea then proceeded to let Julie know all the things she had done over the years that had hurt Andrea. Julie was stunned and embarrassed. *Why would Andrea do this,* she wondered, *especially with Lyndie present?* Andrea spewed her vengeance on her former friend until the waitress reappeared with their lunches. Julie excused herself and went to the restroom, where she hid in a stall.

Nauseated and shaky, she tried to get a grip on herself. Finally, she scribbled a note saying she had to leave, slipped it to their waitress, and headed for the shelter of her car. After fumbling with her keys, she put the car in reverse and backed into the curb. She then burst into tears and sobbed all the way home.

Later, Julie replayed the day in her troubled mind. She felt so betrayed. She had no doubt that she had made mistakes in their friendship, but the lunch had turned into a barbecue, and guess who was on the spit? Julie decided the reason they had chosen a restaurant on Lyndie's side of town was to give the tag team an emotional advantage. Ganging up and then catching Julie off guard seemed to give Andrea the leverage she wanted.

Julie wasn't sure she could ever forgive Andrea. She certainly never wanted to see Lyndie again. Pictures of Lyndie's nodding head, arched eyebrows, and sneering gaze kept returning to taunt Julie and cut deeper into her wounded heart.

We have all been hurt by someone. And no doubt we have all hurt others. But that pain is deepened by deception and hidden agendas.

Andrea and Lyndie had carefully planned this "visit." Andrea had talked through what she wanted to say about Julie to Lyndie. And Lyndie had lavished her approval, support, and even assistance on Andrea to sharpen her strategy.

Julie's experience reminds us that deception is a lie shrouded in secrecy, while a hidden agenda is a controlling scheme, a distorted plan, a treacherous tactic. Deception plus hidden agenda—hmm, this is beginning to reek like an ancient foe—you know, the one with the pitchfork, Satan.

Sometimes I need to be reminded of Satan's deceptions and hidden agendas, not only because they hurt me—even more deeply than Julie was hurt—but also because I soon forget his long-term commitment to my destruction. Understanding that Satan is the author of hidden agendas, that his language is lies, and that his motive is our demise prepares us for his attacks.

This enemy seldom shows up in his flashy red suit with his stubby little horns gleaming in the sunlight, announcing his plan to bump us off. Instead he camouflages himself and appeals to our longings and lusts.

Satan wants us to hide in inappropriate places, for he knows it will increase our dissatisfaction with ourselves, others, and life in general. We then become disillusioned and candidates for despair. That's all part of his hidden agenda.

Strategist that he is, he doesn't limit himself to corrupting our hearts toward our friends. He also lures us into his shadowy hideaways through seduction, and sometimes an observer can spot his techniques much more readily than Satan's prey can.

When the handsome young man stopped at my airplane seat row, I couldn't help but notice the bouquet of wrapped roses he placed gently in the overhead bin. He sat down and extended a warm smile in my direction. By the time we were airborne, we had begun to chat. He told me the flowers were for his expectant wife, who would be waiting for him when we landed. They had been separated, and he had decided to be reconciled with her. Seems he had gone on a business trip and just never returned.

I said I thought his decision to go home was an honorable choice and that it was wonderful he would be with his wife for the birth of their first child.

He asked if I was traveling for business or pleasure. I told him my business *is* a pleasure. I explained that I speak to women regarding their emotions from a Christian perspective. I then expected him to lose interest. Instead, however, he seemed eager to hear more. He asked me one question after another about the Lord and the Bible. He seemed to be a man tottering between two worlds, undecided about which way he would go.

Then it happened. Ms. Beelzebub herself came slinking down the aisle. Actually, she was an attractive gal, but she was certainly older than my seatmate. She stopped at our row, leaned down, and softly purred into his face, "I wish I had someone to talk to." She tilted her head, flashed her extended eyelashes, and then gave new meaning to the word *turbulence* as she swished her way to the restrooms in the back.

The young man almost suffered whiplash when he

twirled around to see where Miss Hospitality was going. He continued to talk to me, casually now, as he kept one eye glued on the aisle.

Soon she wiggled back and announced her availability to him with a promising nod. Within moments, he excused himself from our visit and galloped to her row. I noticed they bought some drinks from the flight attendants and were soon drowning in each other's company. With heads together, their laughter sporadically filled the cabin. My heart filled with sadness.

Just before landing, the young man returned to his seat and avoided my glance. Then he said, as if to no one in particular, "I'm sorry we couldn't finish our talk."

"We could have," I responded kindly. He didn't answer.

When we landed, I deplaned ahead of him. After greeting Les, I pulled him to one side to observe the man's homecoming.

I spotted a pretty pregnant girl watching on tiptoes as passengers disembarked. I figured she was the one waiting for her runaway husband to return to her. Then he appeared. The young woman rushed into his arms.

The seductress walked past the couple and then turned toward them. The foolish fellow drew his wife into his shoulder, and while her teary face was buried in his shirt, close to his heart, he waved behind her to his departing "friend." The temptress smiled coyly and waved what apparently was his business card, as if to remind him she would be in touch.

Talk about seduction and hidden agendas! This flirty female had truly played the devil's advocate, and the young man had taken the bait hook, line, and, well, you get the picture.

***

Actually, fishing is a good way to understand Satan's hidden agenda for us. I come from a long line of fishermen, the kind who won't let you move around in the boat lest you disturb the fish. Some of my kin have been known to sit in a rickety rowboat 24 hours at a stint. They sit and watch for activity in and on the water. When the action is right, they cast out, hoping to snag a whopper. When the fish takes the bait, he's reeled in and soon becomes dinner.

In much the same way, Satan slips his rowboat into the waters of our lives. Then he waits for our moments of weakness, watches for our unmet needs, and lurks in the murky, unsettled issues of our lives. He carefully checks his tackle box and selects just the right bait. When he thinks the time is ideal, he casts his line and waits for as long as necessary for us to take the bait. Then he reels us in with hopes of having us for dinner, and not as his guests. Unlike the fishermen I've known who return the small fish to the water, Satan never throws any back. In fact, he seems to favor the little ones.

Part of his lying agenda is to lure our children into his pond. He knows that if he can reel them in when they're young, he will hold a hidden advantage to use against them when they're older.

If snagging us when we're young doesn't work, he waits for misfortune or affliction to befall us and then tries to lure us into his cove to take shelter from the hardships of life. The water there is diseased, and in his polluted pool we become stagnant. We stop growing, we lose our vitality, and we begin to die. Meanwhile, Hook sits in his dinghy and guffaws.

———————

Samson was a man who loved living on the brink of danger. Of course, he eventually fell over the edge . . . straight edge, that is.

Satan sharpened his strategy to fit the weakness of Samson and his beautician friend, Delilah. Cunning creep that he is, he used a woman's coquettish ways to seduce the big boy. Then Satan dangled a bag of jingly coins to entice Samson's girlfriend. The devil knew their susceptibility.

When I tell you Satan runs a clip joint, I'm not kidding. Samson went in looking like Sylvester Stallone and came out sporting a Telly Savalas coiffure. Motivated by money, Samson's mistress gave him more than a crew cut—it was a shrew cut!

Satan's hidden agenda was to use Delilah to shorten not only Samson's locks, but also his life span. Seduction was Samson's hot button that the enemy pushed, and the result was a reduction when Samson's muscles turned to mush.

Samson gave away his hair-itage to a hidden agenda

Psalms 13

Look at me, o dad my God,
and answer me. Restore
my strength; don't let
me die.

Don't let my enemies say
"we have defeated him";
Don't let them gloat over
my downfall.

I rely on your constant
love; I will be glad,
BECAUSE YOU WILL RESCUE
ME! I will sing to you,
o dad; because you
have been good to me.

AMEN

Mathew 4: 23, 24
"But I will restore you to health
and heal your wounds," declares
the LORD.

Psalms 27

The Lord is my light and my salvation, I will fear no one. The Lord protects me from all danger.

I know that I will live to see the Lords goodness in this present life.

TRUST IN THE LORD HAVE FAITH, DO NOT DESPAIR, TRUST IN THE LORD

Exodus 23:25

Worship the Lord your God, and his blessing will be on your food and water. I will take away sickness from among you and suffered with a blinding rage. When his captors brought him into their celebration to make light of him, he had his own agenda. Appearing to need a pillar to lean on, he became a smashing success when he literally brought down the house with his farewell performance.

This Bible story is a portrayal of betrayal. It shows us the ways of Satan, that wily weasel, and how he lures us by our lusts into dishonesty with ourselves as well as others.

Hidden agendas are tricky plots. Some are hair-raising, some are heartrending, but all are destructive.

As if this picture of Mr. Deception isn't distressing enough, add to it his ability to ensnare us with lies. "Liar, liar, pants on fire" is an accurate description of Beelzebub, old hot britches himself, with his incantations of incriminations.

"What's the matter, dummy, can't you do anything right?"

"No one really loves you!"

"You're so ugly!"

"Stupid!"

"Is this the best you can do?"

"God doesn't love you."

Those are just a few of the ugly utterances he whispers and sometimes shouts at us. As we learn how to detect his lies and schemes (by knowing the truth), we protect ourselves from his hidden agenda.

Josie knew, at four years old, that she should not

touch the pretty vase on the coffee table, but this day the sunlight caught the patterned glass and set it aglow, making it irresistible. She just wanted to hold the sparkling treasure for a moment. When she turned to set it back in place, she heard her mother's footsteps and hurried to move away. The vase wobbled and then tipped to the side and toppled to the hardwood floor.

Josie's mom stepped into the room just as her heirloom shattered. Before Josie could speak, her mom grabbed her by the shoulders and shook her repeatedly, yelling, "You bad little girl! You bad little girl!" When her mom let her go, Josie ran to her room and hid under the bed.

In the meantime, Mom had pulled herself together and felt terrible about her strong reaction and cruel words. She pulled Josie out from under the bed and held her close. "Josie, I'm so sorry. Please forgive me," she said. Then she wiped away Josie's tears. But she was unable to wipe away the indictment.

Josie was relieved her mom wasn't angry anymore, but her mommy's words kept playing in her head as she fell asleep: "You bad little girl!"

The enemy had waited for a vulnerable moment. He placed the scene in his fishing box with plans to "tackle" Josie by casting her mother's line again and again throughout Josie's life, for he knew her susceptibility to it.

As an adult, Josie found that even the least failure on her part filled her with shame. In talking this through and pinpointing the still-painful vase memory, she realized she needed to forgive her mom for responding unkindly. She also needed to forgive herself, not for being inquisitive but for being disobedient. After that, whenever the enemy taunted her with "You bad little girl," she was free not to be drawn into his cove.

Because Josie had initially taken the bait, Satan had then fed her other lures from his assortment of lies. She would need time to sort through her beliefs about herself and untangle his twisted lines. Josie believed she was bad and had acted out of that conviction. Her poor choices included unwise relationships, which also needed to be examined and corrected.

Andrea's unforgiveness, the young husband's unfaithful nature, Samson's unyielding spirit, and a child's unshielded heart were the ponds that Satan found to dangle his crooked hook in. When each of those people bit, he snagged them with betrayal, seduction, and condemnation, all results befitting his hidden agenda.

But Josie found there is One who came to make the crooked straight and to bring light even to the corners of a child's wounded heart. When she stepped from the shadows of the cove, she found safety and acceptance in His harbor. She learned of His heavenly agenda and His plans for her.

" 'For I know the plans that I have for you,' declares the LORD, 'plans for welfare and not for calamity to give you a future and a hope' " (Jer. 29:11).

HURTING

Chapter 5

Hurters

Stacy still remembers the day she reached into the cereal box to find the toy prize for her children and instead extracted a live mouse. Not only did she throw the box a country mile, but she also began to throw everything else within reach. She had had it.

Nothing had gone right for a month. Her youngest had chipped his tooth, her oldest had flunked his finals, her husband had been laid off from his job, and now a lousy mouse was chomping on the Cheerios.

Her kids didn't know what to think when cans, cups, and bowls all became airborne. This was their mellow mom? As the Windex bottle ricocheted off the TV and knocked the lamp off the end table, the kids headed for higher ground.

The shattering of the lamp stopped Stacy's stampede and set off an avalanche of tears. She cried so hard that the children risked coming back into the kitchen to see if they could comfort their distraught mom. Their efforts were to no avail, and soon all of them were in tears.

Paul, Stacy's husband, returned from the store to find shards of glass, dented cans, and a sobbing family. He was stunned. After he pieced together the story, he carried his depleted wife into their bedroom and tucked her in bed. Then he swept up the debris, assured the children all would be fine, and went in and sat on the edge of the bed to comfort his wife.

Even though this was out of character for Stacy, Paul was certain a good night's rest would put things in perspective and get Stacy back in sync. After several sullen, lethargic, tear-stained weeks, however, he realized they might need outside assistance.

Counseling helped Stacy and her family to understand that the mouse was the proverbial straw and the shattered lamp was a picture of Stacy's emotions—painful emotions she had carefully tucked under her easygoing ways. In much the same way that Paul had restored order to the kitchen, Stacy, in time, set things in place emotionally.

Pain comes in packages of all sizes. There's the pain in the neck that comes from having younger siblings (even when we really do love them). Some jobs are a pain, not to mention certain bosses. Yet to be without work adds its own emotional pressure. There's the pain that pierces our heart when we lose someone we love or the pain like Stacy's that can accumulate for some time and eventually becomes too much to bear. Whatever size the package, none of us escapes life without her share of pain. The question is not so much do we hurt, but what do we do with our pain?

Working through the hurting section of this book will be like emptying an overstuffed closet or sweeping an unkempt room. It will be a hard task, but the results will be worth the effort.

We'll begin by looking in the next chapter at how it feels to be a hostage to our pain. In the following chapter, we'll take a peek at how we become controlled by our hostilities. And in the last chapter of this section, we'll examine why we get tripped up by other hindrances. Most importantly, at least to those who are hurting, we will consider the way out of our emotional eruptions.

Chapter 6

Hostages

Joseph's brothers thought they had pulled a fast one when they ditched their younger sibling and then sold him into slavery.

I think the jealousy between them started with Joe's new coat. It left his brothers seeing colors—shades of green and raging red. Things escalated when Joe told his family about his dreams of superiority, which set off more rivalry and led to their hostility and trickery.

Joe's dreams of sheaves turned into real-life shoves when his kin pushed him first into a pit and then for a pittance sent him to Potiphar's home, where he eventually landed in the pen.

He was actually doing quite well working for Potiphar, the Egyptian captain of Pharaoh's bodyguard. The problem was Potiphar's wife, who thought she should be guarding Joe's body. Contention soon turned to detention when Joe was stripped of his position (not to mention other necessary items) and sent to prison.

Here was a young man who understood what it is to be a hostage of other people's hostilities. How painful for Joseph to realize his own brothers wanted to eradicate him from their family line. How difficult it must have been to have his boss's wife pawing him, demanding what he wasn't willing to give—his integrity as well as his virginity. How dreadful to serve out a prison sentence when he hadn't done anything wrong. Everyone else had decided Joseph's future, which seemed to leave him a victim of their vices.

Have you ever had to go somewhere you didn't want to, to spend time with someone you didn't like? What a strain! Now add to the picture the pain of finding out once you arrive that your host doesn't plan on letting you leave . . . ever! His strategy is to eliminate your freedom and work out his wicked intentions toward you. You are trapped in your misery and his mastery. You have become his hostage.

That's how Joseph must have felt. And that's how it feels to be a victim of a painful past, a powerful person, or panic attacks—there is no way out, and you will never leave this nightmare.

A panic attack holds us hostage through fear. It's an assault on the body often generated by our fragile emotions. Panic leaves us confused and vulnerable to the enemy as he hisses lies in our direction. His plan is to keep us hostage by fanning our fear.

In my attempts to describe a panic attack, the word *flush* comes to mind. Not flush as in embarrassed but flush as in toilet. A panic is like repeated flushes, not of water but of terror. This terror surges through your entire body.

Imagine your heart banging against your chest while your mind stampedes wildly. Then a quaking in your hands drops suddenly to your knees, leaving you weakened. Someone then backs onto your chest with a Mack truck, while another person shovels sand into your lungs. Sustain those feelings for a few minutes and you have your basic panic attack. If you haven't had one, I don't recommend it. It isn't a comfy spot to hide out emotionally.

My first panic followed an argument with my husband, Les. It hadn't even been a big fight. But when he turned to walk away, somebody flushed. I couldn't breathe. Les rushed me to the hospital, where I was given a shot of Demeral that knocked me out. My bewildered husband took me home, and I slept off the attack. When I awoke, I felt emotionally dazed and physically drained.

I remembered in the emergency room overhearing two nurses laugh because I had this spell following an argument with my spouse. Their laughter drenched me in shame. I didn't understand what had happened to me, and I certainly couldn't find any humor in it. I was sure the physical surge of panic was an impending sign of death, and my frenzied emotions seemed to support that theory.

Following this episode, I went to my family doctor, and he increased my tranquilizers. That led me to believe the panic was all my fault and that the laughing ladies understood the joke was on me. Now I wasn't sure what was going to happen first—would I lose my mind or die? Death seemed safer, even though I very much wanted to live.

I remember thinking I must be allergic to my anger since the panic attack followed an argument. So I buried my anger deep within, and what came up in anger's place was unreasonable fear. Instead of easing my problem of panic, the fear fed it.

My circle of life was drastically altered as the panic flushing continued. At first, I blamed places and people for triggering this reaction rather than understanding the turbulence originated from within me and my ineffective ways of dealing with hurt.

In time, I narrowed my existence to the four walls of my home. I spent the next two years trying to pump up the wherewithal to get back into the flow of life. But Fear has friends, and they were crowding in. Fear hides out with Guilt, and Guilt shares his campfire with Anger. Unexpressed Anger then sends her cohort Depression to pay a visit, and Depression drags his in-law Despair everywhere he goes. So my place was filling up fast, and, like company who overstay their visit, my "guests" were becoming unbearable.

I had gone from not wanting to leave home to not wanting to get out of bed. My circle of reference was shrinking. I wished I could have a disease—not a painful or dangerous one, but one that would make my cloistered behavior legitimate to the outside world and allow me to continue refuging in my room. That way I could retain a shred of dignity, and yet nothing would be expected of me by others.

One day it came to me that my life was threateningly restrictive and so dominated by the fear of fear that if I didn't get help, I wasn't going to make it. I felt as if I were going under for the third time.

I once heard Jan Ream, author and counselor, say, "Until our pain level gets high enough, we probably won't change." Notice she didn't say we couldn't change without a high pain level, but she said we probably won't. I've found her insight to be accurate. When my emotional pain level shot up and stayed there, I was willing to do whatever it took to change.

And change I did. Later in the chapter, I'll delineate some of the steps I took. But for now, the important point for you to hear is that mine has not been a microwave cure—one zap and I was well. It has been an ongoing recovery and the hardest work I have ever done.

If you are a panic-attack sufferer, you will need to roll up your sleeves and commit to the task of your own well-being. Others can offer advice, comfort, and medication, which can all be helpful. But until you take an active role in your own restoration, dramatic change will be unlikely.

I wanted the Lord to heal me in my sleep so I could rise up righteous in the morning. Instead, He has been teaching me I need to be involved and responsive in the healing journey.

Healing is a risk because to be healed, we must trust. Those of us suffering emotionally have a broken trust factor that makes healing difficult. We'll consider that factor in the next chapter, but first let's talk about survival skills. How can we manage the dailiness of life in the midst of panic flushes?

A question I have been asked over and over is "How did you deal with the panic?" Panic is like a circle. A panic attack has a beginning and must come full circle once it begins. The size of the cycle depends on our response to the feelings of panic. If we fan the flame of fear, our circle enlarges, increasing the intensity of our emotions and the duration of the cycle.

The following are a few of the favorite lines the tempter spews in our direction during a panic to increase the severity of our attack:

"This is the worst panic you have ever had."

"You are going to lose control."

"You are losing your mind."

"You are going to die."

"You will never get well."

Lies, lies, lies! But how can we know they're lies? Let's test them.

"This is the worst panic." Whatever we are feeling at the moment seems the most intense we've ever experienced, because we are closest to it. This is the worst headache; this is the best movie; this is the most scrumptious dinner; this is the brattiest child; and so on. When we tell ourselves this panic is just another cycle of discomfort, we help to neutralize its momentum.

"You are going to lose control." When we buy into the lie that we must be in control to be safe, we increase the panic's ability to hold us hostage. Most of life is uncontrollable (weather, unforeseen circumstances, people's responses, taxes, etc.), and yet generally speaking, we remain safe.

"You will lose your mind." This lie tells us our panic is caused by a weakened mind. Instead, panic is fueled by our fragile emotions, which feed the mind inaccurate information. Sometimes the mind has been fed wrong information from the outside, and then it conveys the misinformation to our emotions, which overreact. We are not going to lose our minds; we just need to change them.

"You are going to die." Have you? I rest my case.

"You will never be well." Each time we experience a panic attack, our tendency is to negate any growth we have had. If we have an attack after going for a while without one, we think it's a sign we are right back to square one, which is usually not true at all.

Once I learned to defuse the lies, I began to make progress. First, I changed my thoughts during a panic cycle. That's not easy! It feels like trying to ignore a screaming child who is seated beside you on an airplane. But with effort and practice, you can learn to block out the bad information by a repeated act of your will and focus on things that help you to settle down.

I would tell myself, *You have been through this before, and you will make it through this time.* I would insist that my muscles relax as a way to reduce tension and be an active participant in my own get-well program. At first, like a rebellious child, my muscles resisted my command, but as I persisted, they obeyed.

Learning how to implement your own healing strategy will lessen the panic attacks' frequency and intensity. At times you will suffer setbacks, and a more insistent panic will sneak up on you. Remember the enemy likes sick surprises. Don't indulge his lies or his tricks, but draw on your resources.

Call upon the Lord. (Remember who's in control.)

Calm your body. (Relax.)

Collect your thoughts. (Renew your mind.)

Carry on quietly. (Restore your schedule.)

Those of us who have been or are being held hostage by panic are people given to extremes. Finding balance will not be easy for us, but it is possible. For instance, if you talk too much (and you know if you do), develop listening skills.

If you make yourself and everyone else nervous by your anxious rushing about, take ten-minute quiet breaks to slow yourself down. Your body and mind will contest this discipline at first and thank you for it later.

If you are a couch potato, set realistic activity goals for yourself each day. Note the word *realistic,* because with our extremism, we will tend to either overwhelm ourselves and feel defeated or trade in our "couch potatoness" to become busybodies.

When we hide our insecurities behind gabbing, gallivanting, or other emotional indulgences, we impede our progress and coddle our weaknesses. A true retreat is when we find emotional relief. That happens when we disarm the terrorists who hold us hostage. Panic can be conquered by implementing a new strategy, facing our fears, and resolving our inner disharmony one issue at a time.

Joseph had plenty of reason to panic as he found himself rejected and neglected by family and strangers. As he moved from the bottom of a pit to being a pawed slave to long-term accommodations in the penitentiary, he was accumulating a painful past of prodigious proportions.

His life raises the question, "What else could go wrong?" It reminds me of the guy who was recovering in the hospital from the flu. On his way back to bed one morning, he stepped into his bedpan and slid into the hall, crashing into the medicine cart, which dispensed drugs in all directions. The fellow broke his big toe in the melee. A bevy of nurses found their attempts to help him back into bed humorous, and as they giggled, he slid through their hands onto the floor, hitting his funny bone. He grimaced and rolled over onto the foot of one of the nurses, causing her to lose her balance and sprain her ankle. At that point, I'm sure he suspected life was out to get him.

Joseph might have echoed the sentiment. Woven throughout the tapestry of his life were the threads of misunderstanding and isolation—with his brothers, his father, his "employer," and his employer's wife.

Few of us have experienced such extended separation from our families coupled with the added dilemma of incarceration (although I've known fleeting moments when sending my kids to the Big House seemed easier than keeping them at my house). During Joseph's internment, I wonder if memories were not his most regular visitors, memories that tumbled through his cell like circus clowns. The teasing voices of his brothers sneering and jeering at the show-off dreams of his youth may have reverberated off his cell walls. The dreams, which were God-given, probably seemed more like empty vapors in his restrictive world.

Mingled with his brothers' voices, Joseph may have heard his own voice full of regret—haunting regrets of how, in the past, he had flaunted his preferential robe in the faces of his rejected and jealous siblings. Sadness that he sometimes chose to strut his colors like a peacock's feathers, encouraging the boys to pluck his luck. At times, Joseph's cell probably seemed crowded with the intense temptation to blame himself and others for his painful past.

Even though he avoided embitterment, we also note his pent-up pain being released when his brothers were brought back into his life years later. Joseph shed tears that seemed to evoke a storehouse of emotions: joy, anger, grief, and love.

Joseph is not alone. We, too, feel that panic and past pain seem to be in cahoots when it comes to holding us hostage. Sometimes yesterday carries a loaded six-gun and seems to use our tangled emotions for target practice. When it hits dead center, Regret yells, "Bulls-eye!" That's why we need to ask the Lord to protect us with His Spirit when we "visit" our younger years—an exercise we must undertake to begin the healing process.

Without God's protection, we might remember incorrectly and add to our compost pile, or we might remember so clearly that we embrace our right to live in rage. The Holy Spirit is the one who will lead and guide us into all truth, which brings the liberty of resolution. Also, we need a support system (a wise friend, a competent counselor) to help us hear what we are feeling, to hold us accountable to change, and to initially validate us as we grow.

When Ginger first phoned me, she said she suffered debilitating headaches whenever she knew she would have to see her mother. It was obvious her mom-stuff had been stuffed too long as far as her body was concerned. I asked if she had someone she could talk to and pray with regarding her feelings. She said her pastor's wife, Carlie, was a friend whom she trusted and respected, so I encouraged Ginger to meet with her once a week for a while.

The results were painfully wonderful. Each week, Ginger would write letters about the abuse she suffered at the hands of her mom. When she met with Carlie, she would read the letters and then talk about what had happened to her as a child. Sometimes Ginger cried, and so did Carlie. At times, Ginger felt and expressed her contempt for her mom. Eventually Ginger released her right to stay angry, and her body and emotions responded by releasing her head as their hostage.

Ginger and her mom will probably never be best friends, but Ginger now enjoys short visits with her without suffering physical repercussions or emotional roadblocks.

A principle I learned from Lewis Smedes in his book *Forgive and Forget* is that forgiving others doesn't make them right, but it sets us free.

Joseph must have had a full-time job forgiving all his offenders, because the "big" people in his life came on like the Gestapo. His brothers even formed a posse and held him hostage. Instead of lynching him, though, they sold him into slavery, clinching the deal with a bag of coins. (I know kids who would gladly donate their siblings to slavery!)

Young Joseph found his "new life" threatened by his boss's powerful wife. Seems she suffered from attention deficit, and she thought Joseph should be her personal tutor. He resisted, she insisted, and he ended up "enlisted."

She persuaded her husband that Joseph was a jerk, and Potiphar used his influence to have him deposited in the local slammer.

While others determined his outer surroundings, however, they did not have the power to dictate Joseph's inner responses. He stated clearly to his brothers at their reunion, "God sent me before you to preserve life" (Gen. 45:5).

What an awesome reply from a man who had his path diverted because of his siblings' hateful hearts! He suffered deeply at the hands of insensitive people who used their strength to abuse and misuse him. He had evidently wrestled through the injustices of life with the Almighty and realized God was all-mighty and able to use even the treachery of others for his good. Somehow, embracing God's providence in spite of the bullies in this world frees us from allowing their powerful ploys to take us captive.

Joseph's life is an example of how panic and our past are joined in their hostage-taking efforts by powerful people. When we allow strong people to back us into a corner, we become their prisoners. (Joseph chose a physical prison over the emotional jail Potiphar's wife offered him. It's better to be locked in a cell than to drink from another's well.)

Sometimes we feel we must submit to controlling people or risk their rejection. Gratefully, Joseph took that risk and ran for higher ground (and a robe). For some of us, though, controllers have a stranglehold on our emotions, and we haven't figured out how to shake free of their suffocating grasp because we desperately want their approval.

Tom felt nauseated as he stepped from his car and headed toward his house. His temples were pounding so loudly that it was difficult for him to listen to his own thoughts. He felt as if he were nine and had to tell his dad he had flunked a spelling test. Instead, he was 49 and had to tell his dad that he would have to move into his own place.

Tom's dad had come to visit a year prior and had just never left. Now Tom couldn't put it off any longer. The pressure on his wife and children, not to mention Tom's bleeding ulcer, was forcing him to speak up. But it's hard to talk to a tank. A retired army officer, Tom's dad was used to giving orders, not taking them.

Tom tried to clear the fear from his throat. Then, sounding far more confident than he felt, he blurted out the eviction notice. He then steeled himself for the fallout. His dad moved briskly about the room but said little.

In the following days, Tom's house was filled with his dad's stony silence. But Tom felt good about his decision, because he had done what he knew needed to be done. An inner settledness helped him to endure the loss of his dad's approval.

After a week, Tom's dad asked if he would look at an apartment he had found. Tom, relieved his dad had heard him and taken him seriously, was glad to assist.

Changing the direction of an unhealthy relationship is extremely intimidating, because change usually brings confrontation. The "c" word is a scary one for hostages.

But once change and confrontation are resolved (as much as we are able), we feel a deep satisfaction and a healthy sense of self.

Any way you look at it, whether our hostage-taker is panic, our past, or a powerful person, being a hostage is a hellish experience. The enemy would lock us up and keep us there. But our Liberator came to set us free. That doesn't mean we won't experience a myriad of feelings including fear, sorrow, misunderstanding, and intimidation. But we don't have to allow them to keep us hostage. We can learn from Joseph.

The panic Joseph surely felt as a lad being rejected and neglected by family and strangers must have left him shaken. Add the panic to the powerful people and his painful past, and his story gives us an up-close-and-personal look at someone who overcame his worst nightmares to live out his highest dreams.

Chapter 7

Hostilities

"Thar she blows!" I felt like a Mobyette (a female whale spotter) as I stood atop a craggy point and saw my first whale spout. What a kick!

My friend Linda and I were at a seaside park in Monterey, California, while the whales were migrating. We were perched, binoculars in hand, on a high rock, looking out at the Pacific Ocean. The park guide had told us to watch for the spouts. I had no sooner approached the point when I spotted what appeared to be a geyser, followed by a two-pronged tail that waved in the sunlight and then disappeared into the ocean depths. Once I saw four whales spout simultaneously. They lined up like a train, surfaced, and then all blew their tops together.

Actually, that has happened at my house. But instead of whales, it was males. My husband and two grown sons have all lined up and spewed about something. Okay, okay, so I was in the pack— oops, I mean pod (family of whales)—too. All right, the males were the ones shouting, "Thar she blows!" and I was the one spouting. Satisfied? But my pod has spewed a few times, too. So there.

In some ways, Les and I are like two peas in a pod. We both have a lot of dynamics, which is the nicest way I can think of to say we are gifted spouters. We have had to learn appropriate ways to express our anger rather than surfacing just long enough to blow our tops and then diving back out of sight.

We blamed each other's anger on our nationalities until we discovered every other couple does, too. Les referred to my stump-jumpin' fury as being a direct result of my ridge-runnin' Southern heritage. I called him a French dip that had been dunked one too many times, leaving his temper too hot to handle.

As long as we were blaming, we weren't changing, and our unresolved conflict grew in intensity. When we risked change in our relationship, we found we had hidden other important and often more accurate feelings behind our anger. At times we felt misunderstood, inadequate, embarrassed, or hurt, yet we responded temperamentally. We also learned that some of our legitimate anger was being taken out on the wrong person.

It was a relief to learn that being angry was not always a sin. Les and I discovered anger wasn't wrong unless we used it to get our way, to dodge responsibility, to annihilate someone's worth, to intimidate others, or to cover up other valid emotions. We had been guilty of all of those at times.

Scripture warns us, "Do not let the sun go down on your anger" (Eph. 4:26). But I confess I have sometimes taken a bath in wrath. I've soaked in it, lathered up with it, and then splashed around in it. I've lingered in it for days, months, and even years. The result is not unlike sitting in a tub too long—we shrivel up.

We see the signs of a world drenched in wrath. Rape, murder, and other abuse issues are rampant and usually the result of rage on the rampage. How did we become such a volatile society? We are like a global time bomb; can't you hear us ticking?

I'll admit I don't have all the answers. (Don't tell my husband.) In fact, I don't even have all the questions. But as a sporadic spouter, I am learning about my own anger and how to handle it more appropriately. I'm not saying I always do it right. Sometimes I still blow it, or should I say blow up. But like vintage wine (nonalcoholic, of course), I don't pop my cork as easily now.

Probably one of the clearest understandings of my misplaced anger came years after my agoraphobia. Long ago, I read a book (don't ask me the title; I can't remember it) that captured me with one paragraph. It told of a young child who lived in a house that had only one window. One day, someone threw rocks at the window, damaging the child's viewing place. This caused the child's perspective to be distorted and a variety of harmful emotions, including deep-seated anger, to take root.

From this concept, I, with my artistic flair, have developed stick-figure drawings to help others who are struggling with anxiety, anger, and so on. The house represents our lives, and the window represents our only place to view the outside world.

When we want to see out, we go to our window.

From the window, we view other people, and in our limited, childish ability, we make decisions about how they relate to us. (A child's world revolves around himself or herself. Come to think of it, so do a lot of adults'.)

When we wonder about God, we go to our viewing place, look up, and try to understand how He relates to us and we to Him.

One day, a great big person (or persons) comes into our lives and throws rocks at our window. The big person could be male or female, a parent, an older sibling, a neighbor, a teacher, a relative, or someone else.

The rocks represent physical, emotional, or sexual abuse, deprivation—or all the above.

The dictionary defines *abuse* as "to use wrongly or improperly, misuse. To hurt or injure by maltreatment. To assail with contemptuous, coarse, or insulting words: revile."

Deprivation is described as "the act of depriving (to take something away from)."

When a rock, a combination of rocks, or all the rocks hit our window, they affect our ability to see clearly. Now when we look at people, we see them as they appear to be through the damage that has occurred to us, and we feel anger.

When we look up toward God, we see Him as He appears to be through the distortion that has occurred, and we feel anger toward Him for not protecting us.

When we want to know if we have any worth or value, we go to our window to capture our reflection. What we see is a broken image. We then tend to buy into the lie that we have no worth or value.

When the big people who came into our lives were not looking to God for what they needed, they didn't know how to give to us what we needed. When we went to them for direction, protection, and correction and instead were violated in some way, it taught us at a deep level, *It is not safe to trust. If we trust, we will get hurt.*

Now, not only do we have a broken perspective, but we also have a shattered ability to trust. I've found that when I can't trust, I must be in control to feel safe. But people and circumstances are unpredictable, which creates a constant threat to my security, adding to my feelings of hostility.

As an adult, I responded to my shattered window by watching my universe become a small world, which is not to be confused with Disneyland's adorable ride. Mine was more like Pirates of the Caribbean, full of tension, tyrants, and terror. I found myself held captive in my home, harassed by Hostility's family: Fear, Guilt, and Depression. It took time, but I eventually left the cove and found refuge in a safe harbor.

When Terri first called me from Phoenix, she suffered from panic and depression. She was on medication for both but continued to struggle. She hoped I could fax her a solution. I understood her desire for a quick fix. I, too, had wanted *the* pill, *the* program, or *the* person to rescue me.

I explained to Terri that I had some answers, but that they weren't easy or fun. I told her what I said earlier in this book: Getting healthy emotionally is the hardest work I've ever done . . . but also the most worthwhile. I challenged her to pull on her sweats and her Reeboks, because healing is an ongoing journey. Along the way she would find hope, joy, laughter, and even some value in her struggles. Of course, she also risked the likelihood of running into some fears, failures, and hostilities.

In response, Terri told me that when she was a little girl, her father was a strict disciplinarian. Even though she breezed right over that part of her story, a flag went up in my mind.

"If you were naughty as a little girl, what might your father do to correct you?" I interrupted.

"Well, many times he would take me in the bathroom and stick my face in the toilet," she reported without emotion.

Aghast, I told her as calmly as I could that her father's behavior was abusive.

Perplexed and agitated by my response, she said, "No, you don't understand. I was a very difficult child."

"No, you don't understand, Terri," I said. "You have assumed responsibility for your dad's harsh behavior. There is nothing a child could do that would justify that type of inhumane treatment."

Terri found that hard to receive and even more difficult to believe.

When the rock of her father's hostile behavior struck Terri's window, she wasn't prepared emotionally, physically, or spiritually to handle it. To survive, she did what you and I do when we're not equipped for life's hardships—she hid.

Terri took refuge in the rigid shelter of perfectionism. She thought, *If only I could do better, act better, be better, then maybe, just maybe, someone would love me. But I must never let anyone into my hiding place lest that person find out what I'm really like and not love me just as my dad doesn't.*

Terri was not wrong to hide. Hiding helped her to survive. But the childhood hiding place she selected complicated her life as an adult. I believe that, because of children's immaturity and the lies of the enemy ("Your abuser's behavior is all your fault!"), children often choose hiding places that isolate them or set them up for more violation.

Often people who hide behind perfectionism appear to be untouchables. We see them as snobbish, condescending, and sometimes hostile. The truth is they have deep-seated anger and can't risk additional rejection. I call them the "white picket fence folks."

A picket fence looks inviting and hospitable. We are drawn to the perfectionist with her painted pickets in a tidy row. But as we approach her, we run into some problems. The fence has no gate; there is no point of entry. Also, the fence is much higher than it seemed from a distance. On close inspection, the pickets appear threateningly jagged, like an angry sneer.

We back away, confused and disappointed. The

perfectionist breathes a lonely sigh of relief. She believes we would have been far more disappointed had we found out how imperfect she really is. The perfectionist, with her unvented hostility, has driven each picket in like a stake. For her the stakes are high, because exposure throws her back into the painful emotions she felt as a victim. Rather than risk feeling her sadness, which is intense because it has penetrated so deeply into her soul, she lives in emotional isolation.

I met Carolyn at a ladies' luncheon in Seattle. She was the last one in line, and she had waited for an hour to talk to me. She greeted me and then said, "I don't really have anything to say except hello."

It didn't seem likely anyone would wait an hour just to "hello" me. I began to converse with Carolyn and noticed how articulate and attractive she was. When I pressed her on why she had waited so long to chat with me, she insisted all was well. She said good night and told me she would see me the following day at my workshop.

That night, I dreamed that Carolyn was hiding inside a beautiful house protected by a gateless fence. The fence not only kept me and others out, but it also held her captive.

After the workshop, I told Carolyn about the dream. Without hesitation, she said heatedly, "I put a gate in once, only to share my heart with a friend and then be devastated by her rejection." Her rigid posture, tense jaw, and trembling hands betrayed her inner pain and hostility.

"Carolyn, it's a risk to trust," I agreed. "People will fail us. But isolation is not the answer. Insulation is. One of the ways we can insulate ourselves, or have healthy boundaries, is to choose people to talk with who have come far enough in their own emotional recovery that they will not be shocked or offended by our past."

An idea crossed my mind and I added, "Carolyn, let's be friends."

"Sounds too scary," she responded honestly.

"How about putting in a gate and letting me sit on your front porch? We'll be porch pals," I suggested.

"How do we do that?" she asked with guarded interest.

"We will correspond, and as you feel safe, you can tell me about your life."

That was seven years ago. Carolyn and I gradually graduated from porch pals to parlor pals and now forever friends. Both of us are able to talk freely with the other. Carolyn eventually revealed her secret of sexual abuse. When she saw I was not going to reject her and that I genuinely cared, our friendship deepened.

Carolyn's method of dealing with her past was to fence herself in with her secrets. Her pain was other-inflicted, but her isolation was self-inflicted as she eliminated the gate and sharpened the pickets.

To have ripped the fence down would have been the opposite extreme, leaving her open to anyone and everyone. Boundaries are necessary for healthy relationships.

There could even be times when removing the gate and putting in pickets is necessary to protect yourself from an aggressive intruder.

But once the fence is erected, it staves off friend and foe alike. It isolates us from relationships and from emotions like joy, peace, and a sense of well-being. The anger Carolyn held inside had become a fierce companion. It caused her bouts of depression, self-consciousness, and occasional misdirected outbursts of rage. The thunderbolts of her biting criticism, directed at herself, had punctured holes in her self-esteem.

Carolyn and Terri needed to vent their feelings (with a trusted friend, support group, or counselor) about the ones who misused them and to work through steps of forgiveness (journaling, prayer, and confrontation). But they also needed to give up their "kiddie klub house" of perfectionism that prevented them from having honest relationships as adults. Their pretending and hostility had left them lonely and exhausted.

Les and I came into our marriage with anger issues, and then we kept lighting each other's fires. When we weren't setting off each other's old issues, we were adding new kindling. We couldn't get too close to each other lest we get scorched. It wasn't until we sought the safety and warmth of the Lord's love that we learned ways to douse our own flames.

We discovered the Lord is not taken aback by our

hostilities but instead takes us back . . . to Calvary. There He suffered the impact of a cruel and torturous cross. He knows about rock throwers, abuse, and pain—and the anger such treatment causes. On the cross, He paid the price for our hostilities and provided the way for our freedom.

When we enter the sacred sanctuary of His company, we find He nudges us toward new steps of growth and healing. First, He encourages us to see our rock throwers for who they are (fallible human beings) so that we might conclude those chapters of our lives. Then He moves us to current events as He requires us to take responsibility for our self-protective behavior. That behavior separates us from what we need to do—stop sheltering behind our control mechanisms, the blame game, and our hostilities.

But it's scary to dismantle our hideouts. I'm thankful that He understands our hesitation and insecurity. The Lord doesn't ask us to give up our hiding places without offering us a permanent place of refuge . . . under His wings.

Sometimes, as we walk through our issues, we find out we're furious with God (though we seldom admit it) because He didn't prevent painful events in our lives. A poem by Jessica Shaver was placed in my hand several years ago, and I have carried it in my Bible ever since to read aloud at retreats. Jessica conveys honestly her need to make peace with God in this poem titled "I Told God I Was Angry":

> *I told God I was angry;*
> *I thought He'd be surprised.*

*I thought I'd kept hostility
quite cleverly disguised.*

*I told the Lord I hate Him;
I told Him that I hurt.
I told Him that He isn't fair;
He's treated me like dirt.*

*I told God I was angry,
but I'm the one surprised.
"What I've known all along," He said,
"you've finally realized.*

*"At last you have admitted
what's really in your heart:
Dishonesty, not anger,
was keeping us apart.*

*"Even when you hate Me,
I don't stop loving you.
Before you can receive that love,
you must confess what's true.*

*"In telling me the anger
you genuinely feel,
it loses power over you
permitting you to heal."*

*I told God I was sorry,
and He's forgiven me.
The truth that I was angry
had finally set me free.*

When we express and confess our hostility toward the Lord, it brings down any barriers we've placed between us and the only One who can give us relief, comfort, counsel, acceptance, and the joy of intimacy.

Chapter 8

Hindrances

After years of hearing about Weight Watchers, my turn came to do more than watch my weight balloon. The winter had been especially cold, and thinking I was a walrus, I had put on extra layers of fat to see me through till the thaw. But the snow had melted, and my added coverage had not. In fact, it hung like water-filled saddle-bags from my midsection. I was starting to waddle, which got on my nerves. It takes so much longer to get anywhere when you slosh from side to side.

When I arrived at my first Weight Watchers meeting, I knew I was in trouble. The other attendees were weighing in. I don't do scales. I don't want to know what I weigh. I don't have to know how much to know I'm too much. My splitting pant seams, my "awesome"-sized panty hose, and my hubby's giggles when I donned my nightie were all the clues I needed. Of course, the fact that my nightie could serve as an awning for our front porch didn't help. Actually, I bought it gigantic because in comparison it made me feel small, which is all part of the strategy when you're in denial. Don't change yourself; instead, change your underwear (which my mother told me I should do anyway).

At any rate, I'm sure I have the record for the shortest stint in that organization's history. One look at the scale (have you seen the size of that puppy?) and I was history. I went right to the candy factory to celebrate my ability, even under pressure, to retain not only my unnecessary weight, but also my weighty denial.

Hindrances are things that tend to trip us up. Remember the little boy at school who was constantly sticking his leg into the aisle in hopes he would send someone tumbling? He was a hindrance.

Hindrances can be small and impersonal like lost car keys, or they can be bigger and more personal like my extra weight. Hindrances can also be barricade-size, creating a constant obstacle course in our lives. One of the taller hurdles we will have to scale (there's that word again) to be healed is denial. Of course, having to high jump our defensiveness is no easy matter, either. And watch out for the quicksand of the double bind: You can be up to your elbows before you know it.

Let's lace up our high-tops and climb those hindrances so we can truly run the race.

———◦••◦———

Defensiveness is a roadblock to becoming emotionally healed. I know; it has certainly held me back.

A number of years ago, I joined a troop of friends to attend a convention in Chicago. For fun, one of our friends handed out round, shiny dots that we were to press onto our hands. This circle supposedly would change colors according to how healthy we were. We giggled as all the spots changed from black to sea blue to vibrant green . . . that is, except for mine. Mine remained midnight black.

One friend, in her desire to help me out, held my hand to warm my circle and give me some color. Within moments we looked down, and all the color had drained out of her dot, leaving it dingy gray. She released my hand to examine her fading dot, and before our eyes it returned to a beautiful blue-green.

We laughed at my lack of color and my ability to be a drain. Then one friend looked at me and said, "All kidding aside, Patsy, I see how you struggle with your health, and I think my nutritionist could help you."

"I've been to plenty of doctors," I shot back defensively. "Their cures are worse than my ills." Anger and embarrassment surged through me. But even the flow of hot emotions didn't change the bleak beacon on my hand.

My friend, not put off by my displeasure, pursued her

train of thought. "When I first went to this doctor, my energy level was low, and she helped me with a diet and vitamins. Why don't you give her a try?"

All heads turned in my direction. I felt uneasy and misunderstood. I had tried plenty of routes to health throughout the years without any lasting results. I had finally decided it was just my lot in life to be a sickee, an anemic-looking, wimpy whiner. My friends were all healthy gals who I felt couldn't grasp my dilemma. They had never walked a mile in my orthopedic moccasins. I took a breath and muttered something about not being able to afford a nutritionist even if I had wanted one.

In frustration, my friend said, "Patsy, I have always found you to be teachable until we get on the topic of your health. Then you shut down and move away from any possible resolution. It's almost as if you've closed the door on hope and resigned yourself to never being well."

Hot tears stung the corners of my eyes. Trying to hold myself together, I accused my buddies of not understanding. They dropped the topic, but I retained my anger. In fact, I held onto it tightly. The first chance I had, I rushed to my room to escape the company of my friends and release my pent-up feelings.

I burst into my room and into tears. I stomped around and talked aloud to the Lord about my accusers. Then I picked up my Bible and dropped to my knees next to the bed. Through the tears over my unjust treatment, I looked down at my open Bible. Like a neon sign, these words lit up: "Sing a new song" (Ps. 144:9).

I dabbed at my tears to clear my vision and looked again. "Sing a new song." The words broke through my wall of denial and defensiveness, causing me to consider my friend's insight. I realized I had closed the door on hope.

"Sing a new song."

"But how, Lord?" I asked aloud. "I don't even hum well."

An idea came to me, and I took the hotel notepaper and wrote an apology to my friend for my angry resistance. Then I asked for her doctor's telephone number.

That was 11 years ago at the time of this writing. Today, thanks to Dr. Starr's compassionate manner and wise insights, I'm humming along, doing better than I ever thought possible.

Defensiveness and denial are like twin boulders that create walls. My rock-hard resistance initially prevented me from being able to hear, much less embrace, the truth. Ever try to listen through a rock?

At various times in our lives, we either throw rocks, carry them, or both. The heavy hindrances of defensiveness and denial keep our inner conflict weighed down and covered over so that even we do not recognize our own emotional disharmony. Some of us go through life singing "I did it my way" while feeling picked on, misunderstood, and in an ongoing struggle for control.

Truth, on the other hand, can cause those self-centered behaviors to crumble, leaving room for change.

I remember visiting with a woman named Trish who said she didn't like people who needed credit for everything they did. She referred to a cousin who kept fishing for praise after helping her with a dinner. I could hardly believe my ears. I had never met anyone who needed more applause than Trish. She seemed to require constant standing ovations, which honestly get tiring to hand out. I wasn't surprised she liked being patted on the back; I know I do. But I was amazed Trish was not aware of her exhausting demand on others to keep her pumped up.

Some wise guy once said that if we hate a quality in someone else, it usually means that quality is within us, but we haven't "owned" it yet.

A friend recently mentioned that I'm an intense person. That took me by surprise, because I had never thought of myself that way. I could feel myself resisting her evaluation. I tightened up and uncomfortably slid down in my chair.

When we become tense and uneasy, someone has probably struck a nerve. My response signaled I was about to roll out my boulders to hide behind. Instead, however, I risked thinking through her description and realized *intense* is an accurate word for me. I am intensely happy or intensely sad, and sometimes I'm intensely intense.

Since owning that insight, I can now spot times (lots of them!) when I'm too intense, and I have made an effort to lighten up. Now I think of myself as being on a hot-air-balloon ride. When the balloon starts to fall from intense undercurrents, I drop a few sandbags to lighten my basket and regain some altitude.

Not that I've ever really been in a flying balloon. I don't do altitude. It gives me attitudes. Especially when all that separates me from a free-fall is a basket, a sheet, and a torch. Sounds more like the components for a picnic and a barbecue, which I prefer to do in a park on the grass. To get me airborne, you'll need something with engines, metal, wheels . . . and a long stairwell on rollers that never leaves the ground. The closest I ever got to a hot-air experience was while embracing a bouquet of balloons at the circus. Oops, am I being too intense? Back to my original point . . .

We are unable to recognize the truth about ourselves when we're crouched behind denial and defensiveness. While we're hiding, we feel temporarily safe, but we lose touch with the information we need to change and grow. We can't fix what we haven't faced.

Another hindrance to personal progress is the double bind, a no-win situation characterized by confusion, contradiction, and control. In the bind, we are trapped by two contradictory requests that leave us no way to win. We're perplexed and begin to doubt our ability to reason. We feel too threatened to challenge our crazy-making captor and therefore remain under his control.

Because we moved a lot when I was a child, I had

many friends. I met Donna when I was 14. Donna lived on the next street, and we often ran back and forth to each other's homes. Her dad nicknamed her Tubby because of her generous size. He was always teasing her about her weight, slapping her on the rear when he walked by her, and verbally goading her to go on a diet.

When mealtime came, however, I would watch confused as he loaded Donna's dish with mountainous piles of potatoes and oversized portions of food. Then he wouldn't allow her to leave the table until she cleaned her plate. Many times Donna would plead with him not to make her eat so much because she wasn't hungry. But he enforced his full-plate rule, always adding to her plate, especially starches. After dinner, he would start the tubby talk again.

Donna was in a double bind. She not only couldn't win, but the control he used and the confusion he stirred also kept her strapped into his sick system.

When Jill's husband insisted she find a job to help with the household expenses, she didn't hesitate. With her background in teaching, she was able to work at a Christian school. Halfway into the school year, her husband began to complain that her job was interfering with his comfort. He wanted her more available to him. Every night after teaching all day, she listened to him object to her absence.

Jill felt emotionally worn out by his complaints and gave her notice at the school. After she had been at home for several months, however, her husband resumed his old recital of how she needed to help financially.

Jill was in a double bind.

When we get caught in such a dilemma, we often feel we have a case of the "crazies." To get out of that suffocating cycle, we must pinpoint the bind we're in and then set new boundaries that open up our options so it's possible to come to a resolution.

For instance, if Jill stayed home, she needed her husband to agree to stop his accusation that she wasn't doing her part. If she went back to work, he needed to agree to take greater responsibility for his own comfort and not whine about her lack of availability. He could have it one way or the other, but not both. No more double binds.

We are responsible for our own sanity. We must not blame others for our "crazies" when it's in our control to make healthy changes. We hinder our own progress when we knowingly take part in a double bind.

In the movie *The Mission*, a man kills his beloved brother in a fit of rage. Afterward, he is overwhelmed by remorse and guilt and decides to punish himself for his unspeakable deed.

He is then given an opportunity to serve others who are less fortunate than himself. But to reach these remote people, he must scale a treacherous mountain. To chastise himself for his past sin, he ties a huge bag of weighted debris on his back with heavy cords before he starts the climb.

As you watch the strain and the pain this man bears with every step of his climb, you want to release him from the unnecessary encumbrance of the debris. For it not only holds him back and slows him down, but it also threatens his very existence. Finally, after a number of harrowing slips, with bloodied head, raw hands, and arms gouged by the rocks, he falls into an exhausted heap on the top of the mountain ledge.

A native appears and stands over the man's rock-beaten body. Suddenly the native lifts his spear as if to plunge it through the still form. Your heart wrenches because you know what it has cost the man to get there, and now for him to die seems so grievous. But instead of piercing his body, the native cuts through the cords that bind him, freeing him from his heavy hindrances.

Amazingly, as the man looks up at the native and sees what he has done, he accepts his gift of freedom.

Well, fellow rock climbers, what are you backpacking up and down the craggy mountain of life? Boulders of denial or defensiveness? The jagged rocks of a double bind? Are you tired of holding up your defenses? Are you feeling encumbered by the emotional games of others? There is One who longs to set us free. Christ has already paid the price, but we must be willing to set aside the hindrances that so easily beset us (see Heb. 12:1).

HEALING

Hikers

In this section, I'm merely one wayfarer prompting another to begin the healing process, and for you who already have, to take the next important step. Like all trips, when we can't see around the bend, the long and winding road seems endless. At such points in the path, I find it helpful for someone to extend a hand and cheer me on.

The following chapters are not a shortcut to healing, as much as I wish I could offer one. (I took a shortcut to a friend's house once. I arrived . . . three hours late.) I am convinced that to shortcut this healing journey is to short-change our chances of becoming truly Christlike.

As a foretaste of our upcoming journey, let's travel down the New Testament highway to observe Christ as He encountered the hurting. The first thing I notice with relief is that our Physician took time for those afflicted. Second, He often used touch to transmit compassion (the bent woman, the leper, the man with dropsy). And finally, He always spoke the truth. When we listen to His conversations, we hear Him convey truth through both tough and tender talk. The tough words pierced the conscience and exposed the content of the heart. The tender words penetrated pain and produced peace. He seemed to always have the right word and the right tone for each person.

Have you ever met a hothead? I stayed in a hotel recently in which a high-school singing group was also housed. One of the chaperones evidently had been pushed past his sanity point and began to rant and rave at two of the students in the lobby. He yelled inappropriate comments at one girl and included defamatory statements about her mother. His voice level continued to rise in an obvious attempt to humiliate her publicly. He felt those young people had shown a lack of regard for others and had displayed bad attitudes. This was a definite case of the pot calling the kettle black.

Christ also met His share of hotheads—not only the arrogant, mouthy Pharisees, but also a few patients who were out of control. Yet He had a right response for each. For instance, there was the Looney-Tunes fellow who skipped naked as a jaybird through the tombstones at a local cemetery (see Luke 8:26-27). That guy needed a Physician to help him get his head on right.

Imagine debarking from a boat and being met by a graveside demoniac in his birthday suit. Sounds like material for a very bad dream to me. This boneyard romper was given to seizures of rage until his visit with Christ. Jesus' tough talk transformed the desperate man into a dressed man, one who was clothed in his mind as well as his body. Now, instead of wanting to run madly, he sat quietly at the feet of His Savior.

You can imagine the demand Jesus was in when word spread there was a competent doctor in town. It was not unusual for Him to be pressed by crowds as the well-wishers, the curious, and the needy pursued Him. Such was the day when, in the midst of the throngs, a slender hand sought out the hem of His garment (see Luke 8:44). Immediately, Christ asked who had touched Him. His followers were amazed at His question when it was obvious many had been in physical contact with their Master. But Jesus knew something the others didn't—except for the woman with the slender hand. She knew what had happened: She had been healed, and she began to tremble.

She knelt before Him and told Him what He already knew—her story. Christ gently affirmed her faith and proclaimed her well. That woman with her unclean illness knew she should not have been in the crowds, much less touch anyone. But she couldn't help herself. She, like many of us, had suffered for so long, and the local yokels had only added to her pain and humiliation. Her healing that day came from a compassionate Christ and had more to do with the issue of her heart than the issue of her blood.

Christ spoke tough words of rebuke to the demoniac, and He spoke tender words of affirmation to the diseased woman. He saw their need for a sound mind and a simple faith—and that is what this section is all about. In chapter 10, we'll talk about our need to have a sound mind so we can get a head start on the challenging path before us. In chapter 11, we'll consider our need to be heart smart and take some important steps of obedience. In chapter 12, we'll be reminded that there are some things we can't do, change, or understand, and that those are His parts to take care of.

Jairus learned about His part when, after entreating Jesus to come and heal his only daughter, he received word she had died (see Luke 8:41). How despondent that father must have felt! All hope must have drained from him as he realized it was too late. But Jesus said to Jairus, "Only believe" (Luke 8:50).

When we have done all we humanly know to do, we have no choice but to wait on God. The rock-hard place of believing without seeing holds the potential for great growth in our lives.

As we spend time with the Lord to get our thoughts straight, to allow Him to touch the painful issues of our hearts, and to accept the truth that much of life is outside our control—but not His—we will begin to see measurable progress in our personal journey. Let's continue on together.

Chapter 10

Head Start

I am an eclectic collector. One of my small but joy-inspiring collections is my children's books. For wrapped up inside this oldster's body is a youngster, one who is still exhilarated by the sight of a dewdrop, a ladybug, or a bluebird.

Nestled on my bookshelves is everything from *Heidi* and *Star Mother's Youngest Child* to *Winnie the Pooh*. I love a well-told tale that wraps its story around the child in each of us and gives us a hug.

The *Secret Garden* is that kind of nurturing adventure. Filled with intrigue, sadness, discovery, and growth, this timeless story dances on the edge of our youth yet nudges us into the grown-up world.

When the children in the tale first discover the garden, it's a wondrous find. But not because of its beauty. That was covered by brambles and weeds and would take precious effort to release. The immediate joy came from finally finding what they knew existed and sharing the tangled garden with trusted friends. For the children, the garden held a secret story of tragedy (a young mother's accidental death) and the priceless key to healing (when the children are freed from physical and emotional isolation).

Emotional and relational restoration for adults is like that story in many ways. Some of us hold secrets we have carefully concealed in untended plots in our hearts. Scary secrets, shameful stories, and silent sins. We sometimes sense their prickly presence as they pierce our self-esteem and puncture our relationships.

Other times, our struggles are a mystery to us. We wonder at our lack of color, fragrance, and fruit. When we can't grasp the truth that we are caught in the brambles of our past, walled in by our self-protection and isolated by our keyless lock of resistance, we, like the hidden garden, wither.

To turn the once-lost key is a risk. But entering the untouched garden of our losses and working to untangle our emotions and relationships can release us to flourish.

Does this mean one garden excavation and we're finished? Actually, no. It means that through many weeding sessions, we become current with the Lord, ourselves, and others. After that, it's far easier to keep up with the weeds, briars, and pruning required for our ongoing growth.

In the previous chapters, we have considered the truth that when we feel threatened or overwhelmed, we hide. Often we hide because we hurt and we don't know what to do about our pain. Once we have set aside our denial (yes, I do have problems, and yes, sometimes I *am* the problem), have given up our defensiveness (yes, I am willing to hear what you're saying without fighting for what I deem to be my rights), and have stepped out of the double binds others have put us into (yes, I will take responsibility for my sanity), *then* we can change. Healing can begin. Denial, defensiveness, and double binds keep us from growing. Those powerful *d's* are places we hide when we feel unable to change or are unwilling to do so.

In this section, we enter the path of resolution. We will begin by considering our heads—the way we think—which is often the path to our hearts. We will look at the heart in the next chapter. Sometimes the Lord starts in our hearts and then works on the head. Wherever He begins, we need to respond, and responding often requires relinquishment. To relinquish is to give up, give in, and give over whatever He asks of us. That sounds scary, but it's a pivotal point to establishing a healthy mind-set. When we decide to be His, we become less resistant to the weeding and pruning and more single-minded in our focus on the path ahead. Growth comes down to this question: Are we willing to hear, learn, and change?

———————————

Many years ago, Denise was devastated when a long-time neighbor began to pursue her husband. In time, Denise was served with divorce papers. She had rushes of rage followed closely by paralyzing panic. Denise loved her husband, and she could not understand how that woman could deliberately set out to take Denise's husband, the father of their five children.

Feeling desperate, Denise went to church and knelt alone at the altar. She prayed and cried out to the Lord about the offense. Then something unexpected happened. A memory from her childhood flooded her mind. She saw herself as a young girl borrowing a dime from another girl. She immediately recognized the other girl as the neighbor who had broken up her home and shattered her heart.

Denise felt a strong urge to pay back the dime. She immediately resisted, arguing with the Lord and restating her case of personal injustice in detail. The conviction didn't lessen, however, so Denise ignored it and threw herself into her busy week.

The week weakened Denise. She felt miserable, mistreated, and maligned. She couldn't understand why the Lord was worried about one thin dime when she had been emotionally assaulted with a million-dollar offense. Finally, when she knelt to pray for His mercy and guidance again, she agreed to do what He asked of her.

Denise arrived at the woman's home and reluctantly knocked on her door. The woman answered and was stunned to see her.

Before she could change her mind, Denise blurted out, "When we were little girls, I borrowed a dime from you, and I've come to pay you back."

The woman stared as Denise extended the coin and pressed it into her hand. The baffled former neighbor watched as Denise turned and walked away.

Later, Denise told me that when she started down the steps toward her car, such joy came over her that it was all she could do not to shout. Something liberating and healing happened inside her when she relinquished her right to understand and obeyed God's seemingly outrageous request.

The other woman eventually regretted marrying Denise's former husband, and they, too, divorced. But she never apologized to Denise for her offense. Denise never understood what the dime business was all about. She did say it was the hardest money to let go of, yet it produced the greatest returns she had ever experienced. In the process of letting go of her ability to understand, she found she also loosened her grip on her hurt feelings, her wounded spirit, and her harbored resentment.

An unteachable spirit will lock us out of our own garden. What a wretched thing! Our pain (our secret garden) holds the potential for Eden (our spiritual garden), the paradise of inner liberty and longed-for intimacy. But we must be willing to uncover our hidden garden and allow the Gardener access. We don't want to be like the father in *The Secret Garden* who, because he wouldn't face his pain and loss, sealed off the very place in which he could have found solace.

—◆━━●◗●◗●━━◆—

After we have relinquished whatever God has asked us to, we desire solace. Solace allays the troubled and anguished mind. To be a recipient of God's clarity for my muddled mind, I seek a place of solitude.

How often do you desire to be soothed, cheered, and comforted? "Frequently" is my response. Sometimes friends offer me that type of aid, but more often than not they are busy with many things, distracted by their own needs or incapable of touching or changing my deep inner discord. But there is One who imparts solace and more, much more.

Solitude is an important prerequisite to solace. When I'm flitting, fighting, and forging through life, I don't have the presence of mind or spirit to accept the balm He offers. But when I nail down my hypersandals in a quiet place and lean in to hear His voice and then respond accordingly, I often receive cheer and comfort. Not that I always get what I want from the Lord, but He meets me at my need. It may be only one word, but a word from Him is life, and it sustains me.

I am a people person. I'm a lights, camera, action kind of gal. But I have learned to treasure and even yearn for my alone moments with Him, times when I leave the spotlight of others and sit under the searchlight of His Spirit. In those intervals, the Lord not only consoles me, but He also constrains me. For He knows I need to linger in those moments of light where I meet and retreat with Him.

There I gain a healing level of sanity, a settled sense of self, an inner reservoir of understanding, and a medicinal sense of humor.

It seems like an oxymoron to say we need to seek solitude to recover from isolation. But isolation is like desolation (a desert) to the soul, whereas solitude is like irrigation (a garden) to life. In isolation, I suffer rejection and barrenness. In solitude, I am restored by His acceptance and given the privilege of fruitfulness.

At times our thoughts, like brittle stickers, have to be dislodged when they press against our faith. It's easy in the dailiness of life to buy into the madness of the world—not to mention our bent, when left on our own, to think twisted thoughts. It's in the quiet, as we meet with the Gardener, that He pulls the brambles off our brains. This allows Sonlight in and moves us from being uninformed and misinformed to being transformed and conformed— transformed in our thinking and conformed to the image of Christ.

The Lord consoles, constrains, and at times, much to my consternation, convicts me when I spend time with Him. Not long ago, I attended a prayer seminar in which we were asked to think of our hearts as a garden and the Lord as the Gardener. Then we were to consider in prayer what the Gardener needed to tend to in our garden.

I wanted to place a garden in my thoughts that portrayed my heart. We had planted a small English garden next to our house that was crowded with such flowers as lilies, daisies, sweet williams, yarrow, and hollyhocks, so I pictured that one. I remembered its summer abundance, its sweet aroma, and the delightful array of colors it produced. I liked the thought that my heart was this bountiful garden. I wanted the Gardener to validate my choice, so I asked, "Lord, is this my heart?"

I did not hear an audible voice, but there was such a strong inner impression of "no" that I knew I had picked the wrong spot. Somewhat disappointed, I mentally moved to the front of our home, where we had put in some tidy landscaping. We had planted mostly shrubs, but some flowers were there that made it attractive though not as showy as the other locale.

"Is this my heart?" I inquired of the Gardener.

Again, "no" resounded.

Feeling confused, I remembered that the west side of our home had a scraggly line of ostrich ferns. My first thought was *Oh, no, I deserve a better spot than this.* After a few hesitant moments, I asked, "This is my garden, isn't it, Lord?"

"No" was all I heard.

I thought, *What's left?* Then I remembered a few stray tulips that had appeared at our back fence, and my mind headed in that direction. On the way to the fence, I mentally passed an old, broken shuffleboard slab. I sensed I should stop. I did, and then I heard, "This is your heart." I looked at the concrete chunks, and I began to cry.

Initially, it seemed unkind to guide me to that plot. God didn't show me what I wanted, but He gave me what I needed—a mental picture of my resistance to His cultivation. When I owned that insight, I could then change my thinking about the Gardener's tilling, hoeing, fertilizing, and other necessary tasks. Once I submitted to His gardening touches, my heart's soil began to soften. (I was also encouraged when we had the chunks of cement removed from our yard and found the unused soil underneath rich with potential.)

My life has taught me that conviction almost always precedes cultivation. If I am to be healed, I must be willing to see my true condition.

What does the garden of your heart look like? What must you allow the Gardener to do to tend it?

Another step on the way to restoration is to study the Scriptures. That helps us to develop realistic expectations about our healing journey.

The day I gave my life to Christ, I remember I had never seen the sky so blue or the grass so green. For a time, my world became Eden as I enjoyed my "beginning." I imagined that was how it would remain as I explored one garden path after another, always aware of His presence.

But before long, things began to change. I was still on the path, but at times I would trip over rocks in the trail, and I often felt alone. Eventually, I decided the Lord wanted to use the rocks as stepping-stones that would lead me up to Him. That was a comforting thought, just not an accurate one, because one day I fell into a pit. It took me a long time to crawl out of that deep place of intimidation and isolation. It took even longer to figure out how those occasional, though sometimes extended, pitfalls fit into my relationship with the Lord.

I have since learned that our journey is not an upward, angelic ascent or even a strenuous staircase to heaven. It's more accurately depicted as a trip to the promised land. And I do mean *trip*.

A WANDERING JOURNEY

We would all like to think that our spiritual growth and maturity might proceed something like this:

(a steady, smooth progress) ———— X

Where we are now　X

Most of us, however, do not experience our journey toward God this way. As a second choice, we would gladly settle for a Christian growth experience that would go something like this:

(plateaus of experience, marked with leaps of growth, each lifting us to a higher plateau) ——— X

Where we are now　X

But most of us do not experience growth like this, either. A map in the back of one of our Bibles depicts the journey of the Israelites from slavery in Egypt to the promised land something like this:

The beginning of their journey　X

X

RED SEA

(From *How to Conduct a Spiritual Life Retreat*, by Norman Shawchuck, Rueben P. Job, and Robert G. Doherty [Nashville: The Upper Room, 1986], p.13. Used by permission.)

Check out the Israelites, the weary wayfarers who have gone before us. Thumb through the book of Exodus; it is their travel log and can help to mentally prepare us for our journey. In fact, you may want to get out your magnifying glass and examine the details of their trek. For we will have, like the Israelites, rocky roads and lengthy droughts—not to mention oversized enemies who, at times, seem to tower over our understated faith.

In tough times, I tend to wonder why my garden seems to be withering, why the weeds are growing faster than the blossoms, why the soil is depleted, and where, oh where, is the Gardener.

Having a clearer understanding of my walk with Christ protects me from unrealistic expectations, including the belief that nothing bad will touch me, and allows me to see how, in His hands, all things have value. I have to give up the belief that my life will be an Eden and embrace Exodus as a reality. Otherwise, when loss, pain, and the unexpected happen, I am left floundering with my fragile faith fed by my anemic understanding.

Exodus exposes hardships, plagues, and enemies, but it also encourages us with mountaintop perspectives, daily provisions, and His pillars of protection. Exodus reminds us that we are in transit. This life is not our home. We are sojourners (strangers with no rights of citizenship). When we understand this, we will not be caught off guard by droughts, deserts, or disasters and come to the wrong conclusions about life or the Lord. Exodus prompts us on to the promised land. One day, one glorious day, we will enter His eternal "Eden," settling our citizenship once and for all.

Meanwhile, setting aside our hidden pain, seeking solitude, realistically setting our minds on the path ahead, and searching the Scriptures are ways to protect our thought life and will give us a head start toward healing.

Chapter 11

Heart Smart

Great beads of perspiration blanketed Les's forehead as he sat gripping the arms of the chair. "What's wrong?" I asked, startled by his gray appearance and alarmed by his sweaty face.

"I'm not sure," he said haltingly.

"What are you feeling?" I knelt next to him.

"Numbness up my arm, face, and into my mouth," he reported.

That was Les's first heart attack. He had been struggling with chest pain for a couple of years, but he had been given a clean bill of health by several specialists.

What the doctors decided was no big deal was actually a life-threatening health issue.

After his heart attack, a specialist misread his heart catheterization report and prescribed medication instead of surgery. Les looked terrible and functioned minimally in the months that followed.

Before long, we realized something had to be done. At my urging, a heart surgeon checked out Les's reports and immediately scheduled open-heart surgery.

The four blocked arteries were steadily strangling Les's life away. The surgeon told me that Les would be safer when the doctors took his heart out of his body and held it in their hands than he was without surgery.

His operation was a success, but his recovery was shaky because of complications. He developed adult-onset diabetes, which added strain on his heart as well as turbulence throughout his body and emotions. In more recent times, Les has had two more heart attacks, and his bypass work has begun to block up.

Throughout this ordeal, Les has exhibited a courageous spirit, a lively sense of humor, and a noncomplaining attitude. I find that not only admirable, but also amazing.

It seems to me that some people handle pain and loss with greater dignity than others. I'm an other. If I suffer, I make sure everyone in a five-mile radius suffers with me. Les has shown me a better way.

This is not to say Les hasn't had to make painful adjustments to his dramatic health condition. In fact, he went through a period of grieving, sorrowing over his damaged health, his lost work future, and his restrictive lifestyle. Had Les not faced his loss and grieved, he would not have had the inner space for courage, humor, and fortitude. His disappointment, anger, and broken dreams would have crowded out his jovial nature and his hope for the future.

None of us gets through this life without experiencing loss—of loved ones (through distance, divorce, and death), income, reputation, home, innocence, and so on. But many of us harbor our losses and therefore our grief, leaving us little room for joy or other life-giving qualities. Our hearts become heavy and, if unattended, hard.

After I spoke on grief at a retreat, one of the participants, Mary Hermes, took a quiet walk and penned this poem:

ROCKS

*It seems to me the rocks we sometimes hurl
are unshed tears that harden into stone,
then mount in jagged piles around our souls.
At last we cannot walk through them or see or feel
except the pain of pressing edge.
And then we cast them from us as we can,
praying they do not strike the ones we love.*

When we don't have the strength left to throw our rocks, they become walls.

Jeanie, a pretty 18-year-old, slipped from her bed, grabbed her robe, and ran quietly through the house and out the back door. She reached a clump of trees just before her body wrenched with sickness. Finally the waves of nausea stopped, and Jeanie stole back into the house and to the safety of her room. She knew this would be the last morning she would have to worry about hiding her illness.

Ted, Jeanie's 19-year-old boyfriend, picked her up later that morning for their drive to the city. He nervously reread the hand-scrawled map several times and checked his rearview mirror more often than was necessary. The ride was quiet except for surface prattle and the loud pressure of fearful anticipation. When they arrived at the rickety house, Ted quickly ushered Jeanie inside.

A large, barrel-chested man in street clothes entered the room. He handed Ted a newspaper and pointed toward a tattered chair. He then ushered Jeanie into a kitchen, where she sat down on a wooden chair next to a table. The big man had her hike up her skirt so he could place an injection into her thigh. She was then blindfolded and guided into another room, where she lay on a table.

Jeanie heard the shuffle of feet and unfamiliar voices whispering directions to each other. The cramping began, and soon the ordeal was over. Several people left the room. Then the blindfold was removed. A woman in a floral blouse and tan skirt busily set instruments back in order.

Jeanie's eyes took a moment to adjust to the light, but eventually she found herself staring at peeling paint on the ceiling. The woman handed her a packet of pills and instructed her to take them if she experienced heavy bleeding.

"Where is the baby?" Jeanie asked, lifting her head to see.

"It's gone," the woman said dryly.

"What do you do with them?" she asked reluctantly.

"We flush it down the toilet," the woman answered as she helped Jeanie to a seated position so she could leave.

Ted assisted Jeanie to the car. Somewhere between the decaying house and their vehicle, they made an unspoken vow never to mention, even to each other, what they had done on this cold November day.

Ted and Jeanie married and went on to settle in a lovely New England village. Jeanie gave birth to two adorable daughters and a handsome son. Ted was successful beyond their dreams, affording them finery and financial security. To acquaintances, all seemed idyllic.

But Jeanie and Ted had carefully built a facade around their lives. Jeanie struggled with any kind of honest confrontation, and Ted became sexually involved with many women.

Then something happened that Ted and Jeanie could not hide or deny. Jeanie was diagnosed with AIDS as a result of infected blood received following routine surgery. After the initial shock of her impending death, Jeanie found herself longing to bring closure with her loved ones on unfinished business.

One day, Ted and Jeanie were driving to the doctor's

office when the "Focus on the Family" program came on their radio. The subject of the day: abortion. Jeanie was flooded with her own memories, and she began to pray for courage to speak of the unspeakable. Pushed by the reminder that her time was fading, she blurted out, "We need to talk."

Jeanie had been so guarded with Ted that her intensity surprised him. Out of curiosity, he asked, "Sure, honey, about what?"

The silence broken, Jeanie began to pour out her buried pain, guilt, and loss over their secret baby. Ted looked away but listened to Jeanie's request. She wanted a private memorial service for the baby—just the two of them at the family plot in the cemetery. Ted nodded his head in agreement.

Many years had passed since two panic-stricken young people sought a way out of the result of their passion. Now they stood over an empty plot. Jeanie laid a heart-shaped lace pillow with a rosebud on the ground.

Straightening up, she began to read the tribute she had written:

> *Our little innocent one,*
> *we want to say good-bye.*
> *We've missed the opportunity*
> *to hear you laugh and cry.*
>
> *Because we were so immature,*
> *we wounded you one day.*
> *But God knows we are sorry;*
> *for forgiveness we did pray.*

Tho' many years have passed,
still you linger in our hearts.
Our little, innocent one,
we'll not remain apart.

For when life's battle's won,
our God, He knows 'tis true,
as David did his son,
that we will come to you!

Jeanie and Ted embraced and, through gentle sobs, spoke words of remorse and grief to each other and to God. The barriers between them crumbled as truth and forgiveness mended their broken hearts and relationship.

They named their baby Emily and took the white, heart-shaped pillow home to represent their waiting child and remind them of God's forgiveness.

The remaining months of Jeanie's life were seasoned with deep joy even in the midst of her physical pain. She died peacefully in Ted's arms.

It took an incredible amount of courage for Ted and Jeanie to work through such a tender and tragic part of their lives. Years of unreleased tears and unspoken loss stood between them like the Great Wall of China. For 30 years, they hid on opposite sides of this seemingly insurmountable barricade. Their vigil of silence left them emotionally isolated until finally Jeanie risked the exposure of the secret. Ted and Jeanie spoke the truth to each other, sought forgiveness, and expressed their grief. The wall crumbled.

If Jeanie were alive today, I believe she would encourage us to take bold steps toward resolution. Speaking the truth in love was the turning point for them. It brought Ted and Jeanie out of their refuge of silence and placed them under the protection of God's healing wings.

Jeanie's story reminds us it's never too late to make an honorable choice.

The grieving process is much like Les's surgery. When we allow the Great Physician to examine the issues of our lives, He may need to hold our hearts in His hands. What a vulnerable position to allow someone to scrutinize us that closely and find out what makes us tick . . . and what ticks us off!

Unreleased anguish can, in time, turn to unreasonable anger. That anger, like rocks, can and will block the "arteries" (our relationships) and add to the damage in our hearts.

To become tenderhearted, insightful, and responsive to the Lord and others, we must first wade through our losses. That means a willingness to feel the effects of our loss, to examine our hearts under the tutelage of the Holy Spirit, to release tears, and to relinquish our rights to understand. In doing so, we will feel the pain, but we'll learn appropriate ways to express it. Sometimes it will be through the healing release of tears, prayer, some form of art, or words (spoken or written).

Journaling can expedite healing, because our hands are extensions of our hearts, and many times we will write what we wouldn't risk saying. It's almost as if we bypass our defense mechanisms and, in a safer form of expression, say what's really on our hearts. I don't keep a daily journal, but when I do write, I'm often surprised at what I learn.

During a particularly dark time in my life, I wrote this poem:

WINTER

Winter came early and would not depart,
Winter came early to a tender, young heart.

Frozen inside, the child would not feel,
Locked in her pain, she could not heal.

Icy responses replaced her trust;
Numbed by life's season,
her soul formed a crust.

Hardened by bitterness,
chilled with despair,
Encased in the cold with no one to care.

Icicle tears clung to her face,
Frigid reminders of her shame and disgrace.

Winter came early to a tender, young heart,
Winter came early and would not depart.

I knew I had felt sad, but until I wrote those lines, I had no idea how heavy my heart was.

I took this poem to my friend and counselor Ruth

Ann. We talked about a lot of past and current issues, and that was very helpful. Then Ruth Ann said she was looking forward to the rest of the poem. I wondered what she meant. But one day, after I had talked and walked through many of my losses, I sat down and finished the poem.

SPRING

Spring came late, late in her years,
Spring came late to thaw her tears.

The little glazed sculpture
stood frozen in place,
Till the light of the Son
dissolved her disgrace.

The icicles fell to the ground below;
Her heart, warmed with love, melted the snow.

No longer a statue in an ice-cold rhyme,
No longer a victim locked in a crime.

Spring came late to thaw her tears,
Spring came late, late in her years.

While I chose to express my emotions in a poem, Tonja's journal is filled with expressions of her artistic flair. She drew this revealing depiction of how she felt about all the unspoken secrets from her childhood:

Secrets

The following two journal entries are from a woman and a man in the first steps of personal loss. Judy was an incest victim who was working through her hurt when her father suddenly died. Initially devastated because she could never restore the relationship with her dad, she wrote:

> *He's gone . . . he's really gone. No time to say good-bye. No time to say I still love you. Why? Why didn't he call me and say he was sick in the hospital? He didn't have to be alone. No warning . . . no time to say good-bye. No last hug. How I longed for a hug that felt pure. . . .*
>
> *Now there is no hope. He is gone. The striving is over. But my heart aches for the loss of a redeemed relationship that could have been but never will be here on earth.*
>
> *Daddy, I can live with your death . . .*

*I can live without your presence . . . but
can I live without "the hug"?*

Don struggled with pain and disappointment as he
journaled before his dad's funeral:

> *Lord, you do take care of us. It's been
> so difficult for me, Lord, as I think of my
> dad. Grief just wells up inside of me from
> time to time. It's like a wave that comes
> and then leaves and then comes again.*
>
> *Lord, how special it was to see the
> program with my picture in it in my dad's
> papers. Father, he was proud of me. He
> just didn't know how to say it. I don't
> know if I'll ever get over my relationship
> with my dad. The tether is breaking, and
> I'm grieving over it. This has been hard for
> me. . . . It seems so insignificant to spend
> only two pages writing two days after my
> dad died. I cried for most of the day.*
>
> *Lord, am I grieving two things: the loss
> of my dad and the loss of never having a
> dad? Father, You are giving me insights as
> to what life is all about. Relationship is the
> most important thing we have or do. . . . It
> starts with You and works through all the
> things we do and people we come in
> contact with. I long for better relationships
> with my children and wife and You. It's*

hard. It doesn't come easy for me. . . .
Father, there's going to be so much
emotion tomorrow at the funeral. Help
me, Lord, to get through it.

Whether you express your feelings in a poem, a draw-
ing, or a letter, the important benefit of journaling is that it
gives you somewhere besides inside yourself to carry your
emotions. It also helps you to define your unfinished feelings.

Grieving is a process, not an address. Because we
have experienced loss doesn't mean we should set up
house with it. When we're willing to let the Lord do some
internal surgery and then work through the recovery time,
we will eventually enter the lighter and brighter season of
spring.

Les's health problems haven't gone away, but they no
longer dictate his level of joy. The same will be true of us,
for we will be aware of some losses throughout our lives.
But now the weight is His, and we are no longer emotionally immobilized and stunted. Instead, we become heartfelt
comforters able to extend heart-smart help to others.

Chapter 12

His Part

The long and winding road led Moses high atop Mount Nebo. When he reached the summit, he leaned against his staff to steady his footing and then looked at the vista spread before him. His breath caught in his throat. Stretched out as far as his eyes could see was the land of milk and honey—lush, green, fertile, and fruitful, just as Jehovah had said it would be. Moses' heart palpitated from the thrill of the view, and his eyes flooded with tears of wonder.

Hours passed before Moses stepped back and lowered his ancient body onto a stone ledge. From his seated position, his eyes once again swept across the panoramic scene that portrayed his people's place of promise. Longing sprung up anew in his heart that he, too, might enter the land. He had traveled so far, so very far. But the desire was quickly crowded out by regret. Stinging tears overflowed his eyes and slipped down his cheeks. Moses had not imagined what his fury could cost him.

He leaned his head against Mount Nebo's solid side, closed his eyes, and remembered. Memories of a lifetime moved through his mind. He thought of his mother and how she had loved him enough to release him into the sovereign care of Jehovah. She had done all she knew to do for as long as she could for her baby, and then she had had to trust God to do His part.

Moses wished his mother could see the incredible sight of the long-awaited land. But how would he explain why he would not be joining their people for this part of the journey? "No," he whispered to the mountain, "it's better she doesn't know."

Moses' mind drifted to the palace—the horrible, wonderful palace. Years laced with separation from his family, yet important years of being schooled. And Moses learned far more than was taught. He saw firsthand the habits and practices of the Egyptians, information that would be helpful when he returned to negotiate with Pharaoh. Moses could not have known then how Jehovah's hand was in that palace part of his life, equipping him for the journey ahead.

His thoughts shifted from the palace to Midian and the shrub, the one aflame with the very voice of God. How long had it been since that day? he wondered. Then, without realizing it, Moses slipped out of his sandals. Even the touch of cold stone to his bare feet did not jar him out of his blazing-bush reverie. His eyes dried as if from the warmth of his thoughts. He recalled his reluctant fireside chat with the Lord, amazed at His patience with him.

Then an uneasiness stirred within Moses when he reviewed the mistakes he had made in his life. He wondered if the Lord God had written the commandments on the same material as Moses' head . . . and his heart. No, he didn't have to wonder; Moses was sure of it.

Then the miracles he had witnessed began to flood his thoughts: the pillars of cloud and fire, the wall of water, the food from heaven, the retreating enemies, the tablets, the tabernacle . . . The pictures of God's part passed before him for hours on end. Moses' heart filled with praise until he finally had to release it or burst. In an old man's quivering voice, yet with the gusto of a youth, he sang the song he had sung after crossing the Red Sea. It echoed throughout the mountain as though it pleased its Maker.

Moses stood, straightened his robes, and again drank in the view. The setting sun blanketed the land with shadows as if to put it to sleep. The tears cascaded down Moses' face, but these didn't sting. These tears were sweet like manna. A smile crossed Moses' face, and he sat down again on his high throne of stone. When he pressed his back against the "chair," he noticed how it flared out on the sides . . . like wings. His smile deepened and spread across his heart. Then God showed Moses what He had withheld from him before—His glory.

I can only imagine what it must have been like for

Moses in his last hours when he saw first the promised land
and then the Promise Maker. But one thing I know: There's
nothing like a mountaintop to help us gain perspective.
From that vantage point, we become more aware of not
only our limitations, but also His interventions.

The long and winding road led Hagar to a hot hideout, a desert spot that offered her and her son soothing
sanctuary. There's something about being a "prisoner" that
causes you to value more deeply your freedom. Then hard
times become relative. And a desert becomes an oasis.

I think if we could talk to Hagar, she would not
change one sandalprint of her path. For she not only
gained a son but was also led to the well of the Living
One. When Hagar had nowhere to turn and no one to
listen to her, the God Who Sees saw and heard. Hagar
showed her willingness to accept Him and His promises
when she returned to Sarai's tent. Hagar did what she
could. God did what she couldn't.

How gracious and generous of God to make Himself
known to an "outsider"! Hagar's name would not have
made the "Most likely to chat with Jehovah God" list. She
was the wrong nationality, the wrong upbringing, and the
wrong tax bracket. Yet the angel (thought to be Jehovah
Himself) spoke with her. He drew her into His oasis of
provision.

The long and winding road led Naomi back home. "Home"—what a wonderful word, full of comfort, acceptance, and provision! (That's why our kids keep returning.) But home for Naomi was where she dragged her broken dreams to bury them. She had already buried everyone of importance to her. All she had left were dreams that could now never be fulfilled. When your dreams die, hope becomes the pallbearer, and bitterness becomes your roommate. Ask Mara, "Bitter," the name Naomi assigned to herself as she returned home.

The long and winding road led Ruth to a harvest of hope. She gave up everything she had and ended up reaping all she would ever need.

What was it that caused Ruth to follow her mother-in-law, Naomi, to her homeland? To follow meant a departure from Ruth's place of birth and her husband's place of death—reasons that make most people feel too connected to the land to leave it. Besides, Ruth would have to say good-bye to family and friends, the ones who usually help us survive life and loss. She would leave behind comfortable traditions and known gods to pursue a life of servitude among strangers who worshiped the solitary God.

I wonder if Ruth's husband, Mahlon, had told her stories of his land and his relatives as well as his God? Perhaps that was when a longing began to form in her heart. Or maybe, as she observed the interaction of his family with each other, Ruth was aware they had something she did not. I wonder if Naomi, during better days, was such a winsome woman that Ruth desired to be like her? It could be that Ruth's first encounter with God came through the behavior of Mahlon and his family, and she could not bear to lose that spiritual touch point. Whatever the reason, the results of Ruth's choice leave us breathless.

Naomi's thoughts after the burial of her sons were like a graveyard. Her mind was full of bones without breath and her life without a future. Naomi had said her last good-byes to her husband and sons, and then, with her heart wrapped tightly in grave clothes, she headed home . . . to wait to die.

But her trip was interrupted by an outrageous request by her daughters-in-law, Orpah and Ruth. They wanted to go with Naomi. Couldn't they see she had nothing left to give them? Naomi convinced Orpah to go home, but Ruth refused to leave her. In fact, Ruth went so far as to relinquish her rights to have a future aside from total devotion to the welfare of her dear mother-in-law.

Because she was so full of death, however, Naomi's ears could not take in the words of life spoken by Ruth. They didn't penetrate her pain.

Actually, this moment in Ruth's life was probably in part a result of Naomi's prayers. For Ruth did not just devote herself to her mother-in-law that day but also to Jehovah, the God of Naomi. This was Ruth's conversion day. Yet instead of celebration, she received rejection. But Ruth had not come with her choice contingent on Naomi's ability to hear her. She had come with a mind set on her new life.

Three times Naomi instructed her to return to her own people. Ruth stood her ground. Holy ground. Naomi had no strength left to fight, and Ruth was too committed to give in or up.

The long and winding road led the two women into Bethlehem, where the city was stirred by their arrival. Naomi was honest with her old friends and confessed her emptiness and bitterness. She had gone away with her most precious possession, her family members, and had returned home without them.

Ruth's heart must have been so full of Jehovah that she had no room for offense even when Naomi said God had "brought me back empty" (Ruth 1:21). Ruth had promised to stay at Naomi's side as long as there was breath in her body, and Naomi told everyone she was "empty"? What was Ruth, chopped lox?

Perhaps Ruth realized that no one could replace Naomi's sons. She might have been aware that Naomi needed some seasons at home to heal from her grievous losses. Whatever her thoughts, Ruth continued her focused efforts to serve Naomi and did not allow a slight to become a fight.

Ruth's offer to work in the fields, a difficult and sometimes dangerous job, shows her humble heart and servant's spirit. Her willingness to serve was rewarded in ways that surpassed anything she, her mother-in-law, Boaz, or you or I could have imagined. The harvest from the field produced not only barley and Boaz (a mate), but also a baby. Not only did Jehovah give Ruth a husband and an heir, but also a heritage. Not only did she give birth to a son, but she also became part of the lineage of "the Greater Son."

Naomi's heart began to heal when she saw the basket of barley, then learned of Boaz, and eventually allowed their baby to fill her empty arms. When Mara leaned over to pick up the baby (her part), her bitterness poured out. When she stood up, Naomi's pleasantness returned (God's part).

Ruth took the long, winding road away from all her former comforts, all her hiding places, and took refuge under His wings. She did her part, and He did the rest.

Ruth is a picture of relinquishment. A true sojourner. A sweet-spirited servant. When she turned her back on her former ways, moved from Moab, and headed toward Bethlehem, Jehovah opened a whole new life for her.

Likewise Naomi, even in her bitterness and anger, arose and walked away from the camp of the enemy and returned to the home of her heart and her Healer. Jehovah met her in her emptiness and filled her with the produce of the field and the pleasant fruit of His Spirit.

Like Moses, we have much to remember—years filled with, yes, our failures, but also God's interventions. Like Hagar, we, too, have felt imprisoned in relationships, but God has been our awaiting oasis. Like Naomi, we have suffered unspeakable losses. At times our bitterness has consumed us, and we have lost sight of God's generosity.

We are a hurting and needy people.

But are we willing to be like Ruth? Will we let go of our failures, our sorrows, and our woundedness? Are we willing to walk in His direction? Even one faltering step to begin? Have you pinpointed your hiding places? Are you willing to identify your hurting places?

To assume mental and emotional ownership of our personal pain is to take long strides toward the path of restoration. To take a step is to begin doing our part. God will respond and do His part. He will bring healing.

I don't know where the long and winding road is leading you, but I do know this: If you remember passing Calvary, you are on the right road.

Chapter 13

Finding Refuge
...at Last

We buried my friend's 26-year-old son last week. An accidental gunshot took Jeff's life. We have more questions than answers. We are offended at people who have all the answers and no experience with devastating loss.

I watched the heart-wrenching scenes as the family tried to come to grips with their tragedy. I can still hear the travailing of the mother's anguished heart. I can still see the wrenching of the father's grief-worn hands. I can still feel the distraught sobs that racked the sister's body as I held her. I can still smell the hospital and the funeral home. Memories march before my mind like soldiers, causing me to relive the agony. If it's this difficult for me, Jeff's godmother, how much more magnified it must be for his birth mother! I can't imagine.

As I watched Jeff's mom, Carol, the week after his death, I observed a miracle. I saw her move from despair to hope. From franticness to peace. From uncertainty to assurance. From needing comfort to extending it.

I witnessed a mom face her worst nightmare and refuse to run away. Instead, she ran to Him. When grief knocked the breath out of Carol, she went to the Breath Giver. I watched as the Lord placed His mantle of grace around her and then supported her with His mercy.

The grief process has just begun for Jeff's loved ones. The Lord will not remove His presence from the Porter family. But there may be moments when He will remove their awareness of His presence. That will allow them to feel the impact of their loss. For He knows it would be our tendency to hide even behind His grace to protect our fragile hearts from the harsh winds of reality. He offers us refuge, but He also promises us wholeness. Wholeness means we are fully present with ourselves and with Him. Therefore, we have to own our pain. If we don't, part of who we are we must either shut down, avoid, or deny. That would leave us estranged from ourselves and divided in our identity. Also, we would never heal in a way that would allow us to minister to others.

The God of all comfort does not seem to extend His comfort to make us comfortable. Perhaps that's because our tendency would be to become La-Z-Boy believers, content to crank back our chairs, put up our feet, and snooze through the losses of others. Instead, He offers His comfort that we might be motivated by mercy to tenderly extend kindness to the hurting.

All those who came to Bruce and Carol's house and to the funeral home brought with them two gifts. The first gift was allowing the Porters to feel pain, and the second was sharing the pain with them by their presence. Some, depending on how close they were to family members or to Jeff, would draw out more emotion than others. The closer they were, the stronger the response of pain, but also the greater was that person's ability to support and comfort.

I observed some who came to the funeral home because they could not stay away and yet were fearful to enter into the pain. They stood cautiously on the sidelines and seemed to be testing their ability to approach the family and speak. I watched as they finally risked stepping toward Jeff's loved ones. But before those mourners could speak, sobs filled their beings, and the family they came to help comforted them. The frightened visitors then quickly retreated, exhausted and shaken from the effort.

If we don't feel, weep, talk, rage, grieve, and question, we will hide and be afraid of the parts of life that deepen us. They make us not only wiser but also gentler, more compassionate, less critical, and more Christlike.

We went to dinner with Bruce and Carol after church on a Sunday. Before the meal, we joined hands, and Bruce prayed. It was tender; it was compassionate; it was insightful; it was powerful. I had never heard Bruce pray like that before. It was obvious he was embracing his pain and that God was sheltering him under His healing wings.

Our tendency is to believe we have one or the other, shelter or pain. But I believe God allows us the benefit of both. He does not remove the believer from reality but transforms the realities into righteousness for our welfare and His glory.

My 78-year-old mom came to the funeral home to offer condolences to the family. Carol leaned down to hug her, and my mom said in a voice full of empathy, "I know how you feel; I lost a son, too."

Realization spread across Carol's face as she remembered my brother's death, and with deep emotion she choked out, "Yes, yes, you know how I feel, you know how I feel." I stood by quietly as my mom and my friend held each other and wept tears of mutual understanding.

How healing it is when someone understands us! Recently I wrote a story about a friend and then read it to her. She wept. I asked her, "What are you feeling?"

She replied, "I feel understood—something I have felt so seldom in my life that it leaves me emotional."

There is someone who hears our hearts and understands even our unformed thoughts. Christ is that one. He woos us, and He waits for us to come to Him. With arms outstretched like open wings, He welcomes us. In this life we need a hiding place, and Christ offers us that—a place of comfort, a place of healing, but not a place of painlessness.

There will come a day for each of us when, like Jeff, we will reside where He presides and hiding won't be necessary, for we will be home . . . at last. Finally, we will be in a place where our tears will dry, our pain will pass, our hearts will heal, and we won't ever need to hide again—not from ourselves, not from each other, and, hallelujah, not from the One who knows us the best and loves us the most.

Take a Lighthearted Look at Life
... and Laugh!

God Uses Cracked Pots

No matter what's got you down, this gem of a book will lift your spirits and keep you in stitches. In *God Uses Cracked Pots*, Patsy Clairmont takes an assortment of everyday events and—with punch, poignancy, and side-splitting humor—turns each into a memorable lesson on family and faith. Paperback.

Normal Is Just a Setting on Your Dryer

All of us have things about ourselves that we're not crazy about. But comparing yourself to others is an endless cycle that leaves you all wet. That's the message in *Normal Is Just a Setting on Your Dryer*. Back with another round of hilarious anecdotes, Patsy's collection of short stories is perfect for anyone stuck in the rut of trying to measure up. Available in paperback or book-on-tape.

Pick up these best-sellers at your favorite Christian bookstore.